C0-BKU-052

SOUTHERN PACIFIC COUNTRY
IN THE 1980's

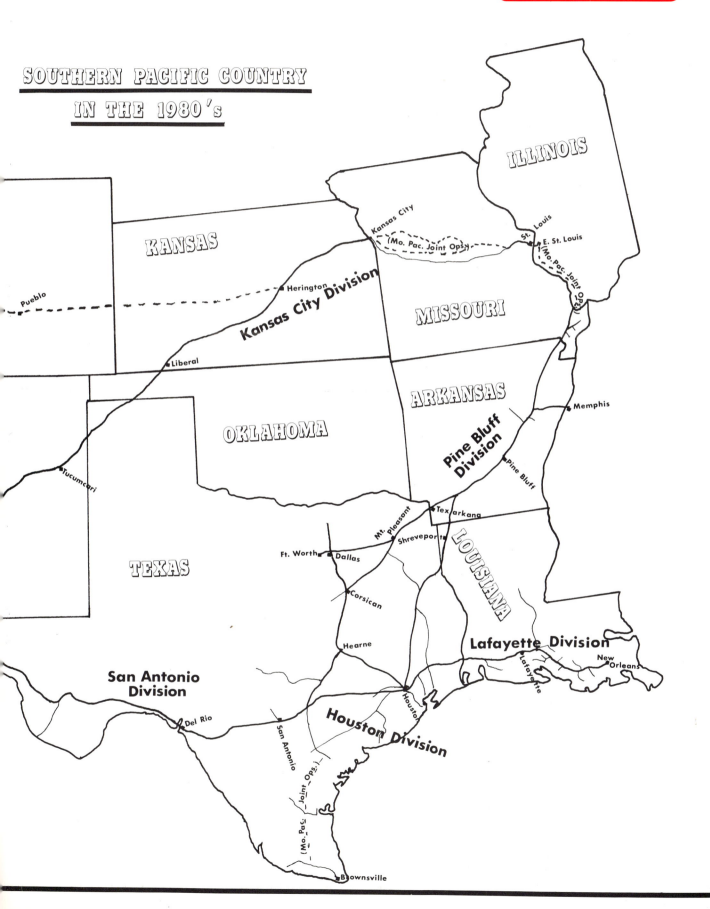

SOUTHERN PACIFIC COUNTRY

BY DONALD SIMS

PHOTOGRAPHS BY THE AUTHOR

TRANS-ANGLO BOOKS
GLENDALE, CALIFORNIA

Front Cover: Having delivered
a train to Phelps-Dodge
Copper Company, a set of
rebuilt 6300s is about to
depart from Clifton, Arizona,
on the Tucson Division.

Back Cover: Light snow
dusts the mountaintops
behind Ogden, Utah, as the
lead units of a westbound
connection off the Rio
Grande tackle mainline iron.

Frontispiece: In recent years,
a familiar sight on Tehachapi
has been the "oil cans," a
unit train that shuttles
between Bakersfield and a
refinery near Dolores Yard in
Los Angeles' harbor district.
The location is between
Caliente and Bealville.

Rear Endsheet: Quick meet at
Tucumcari. The LACHT's
crew is changing while a
westbound freight slowly
drifts out the yard's south end
with its mixed bag of trailers
and boxcars.

DEDICATION

To the patience and understanding of my wife,
Reva Sims.
Everyone should be so lucky.

SOUTHERN PACIFIC COUNTRY

© 1987 by Donald Sims

All rights reserved. No part of this book may be used or repro-
duced without written permission from the Publisher, except
in the case of brief quotations for reviews.

Manufactured in the United States of America

Book Design by Bill Bradley

First Printing: Winter 1988

Published by
Trans-Anglo Books
A Division of INTERURBAN PRESS
P.O. Box 6444 □ Glendale, Calif. 91205

Library of Congress Cataloging-in-Publication Data

Sims, Donald.
    Southern Pacific country.

    1. Southern Pacific Railroad Company.   2. Railroads—
United States.   I. Title.
TF25.S66S56   1987   385'.0978   87-13951
ISBN 0-87046-082-X

CONTENTS

INTRODUCTION

From mountains to plains

_____

AMONG THE GREAT western railroads of the past century, none has captured the imagination quite so much as Southern Pacific. No other steel trail twists so often, tunnels more, nor climbs and descends as many mountaintops as does the broad-brushed map expanse colloquially referred to as Espee. Although overshadowed by the western lines, the eastern expanse is colorful, too, for with the acquisition of Rock Island roadbed, the longtime grey-and-red-trimmed fleet has been scorching mileposts on the Great Plains while continuing to serve the bayous and vast reaches of Gulf Coast country.

Beyond its wide physical diversity, SP has in the latter half of the 20th century exhibited more styles of the diesel builder's art than any other western line, while simultaneously experimenting with whatever operating technique seemed reasonable.

The very fact that this San Francisco-based railroad has failed to be monolithic in form and heart is perhaps its greatest charm. It is, after all, a business and as such is clearly interested in that bottom line which investors and accountants hold so dear. As the 1980s draw to their niche in history, the traditional initials "S.P." etched in white on a prime mover's nose may join the "80s" in kind, and as an independent identity, the name and logo that polish rails from St. Louis and Memphis to San Francisco and Portland may be scattered into barely recognizable segments.

For that reason, keeping tabs on the Southern Pacific in the 1980s has been interesting to say the least. It seemed unthinkable that two such longtime competitors as SP and Santa Fe would even flirt with the wildest dreams of a combination, or that the Interstate Commerce Commission would do more than express a belly laugh at the idea. Yet such had circumstances changed that a partnership almost reached the honeymoon stage. In fact, the cake was baked and the ceremony planned when in a stunning reversal the deal fell through because a higher authority refused to sanction the marriage.

Opposite: Topping the summit after a tough climb up Oregon's Cascades, a EULAY train breathes a bit easier as it goes by Odel Lake.

So back to the drawing board, and as press time draws near the conclusion is still uncertain.

Actually it was never going to be a true merger, more like a submerger of Southern Pacific into a rather unglorious namesake of unwieldy pronunciation termed Santa Fe-Southern Pacific, with definite emphasis on the former.

So much for the compromise locomotive look of the two railroads, which some dubbed the "Kodachrome look."

It wouldn't have worked anyway, at least not on Espee. That bright set of yellow and red hues being spit forth from the shops at Sacramento, Cleburne and San Bernardino would never have proven practical on ex-SP roadbed, particularly west of El Paso. Have you seen any of those paint schemes after six months in the Cascades, or after a winter bucking drifts on the Sierra Nevada uplift? Red and grey holds up much better for longer periods, and in spite of certain rumors, it's not true that SP never owned a locomotive wash rack.

To those bored with the standardization of motive power silhouettes, SP has proven a boon. A few units of just about anything turned out in the '50s, '60s and early '70s turned steel wheels on Espee trails. Moreover, the railroad was the leading element in an experiment to introduce European-style, diesel-hydraulic technology to U.S. rails. Although abortive, it provided an impetus for domestic producers to upgrade their electrical systems—a weak point in early generation units. The California-based railroad also instigated the tunnel motor profile; it tried some double-motored units, and routinely put 10 and 12 units on a single trans-mountain train. SP is still the favored proving ground for new locomotive models.

A flatland hogger probably never experienced "extended dynamic braking" nor should he, but out in the West and perhaps on an eastern coal road the term is routine, particularly where the big red and grey ply their demanding trade.

Roaring flat out with piggyback trade east of El Paso or muscling across great western mountaintops, SP units divide their time between the extremes of gravity, ascending and descending. That they age faster than their brethren on less demanding roadbeds is obvious.

Another SP philosophy, in part dictated by structural form, continues to the moment. It is the long, sometimes heavy and, if possible, fast train. It seems to fly in the face of modern convention and has its share of critics. The phenomenon is to a major degree dictated by the basic single-track nature of the railroad as much as any other criteria. Unlike its western competitors, Union Pacific and Santa Fe, SP does not feature substantial portions of double track in key spots such as Belen–Barstow–San Bernardino or Council Bluffs–Ogden, so track capacity—particularly in the most significant territory such as Los Angeles–El Paso—has always been a fundamental issue to be addressed.

This pattern follows through on most of the Southern Pacific. The profile, which is of single track, Centralized Traffic Control and several-thousand-foot-long movements, does not necessarily equate with slow motion, either, as liberal applications of horsepower—an SP specialty—provide the antidote. Outside the mountainous zones out west this railroad does a fashionable job of moving tonnage at whatever speed steel rail and signal spacing will tolerate.

All that is required is power, and the cue is taken from many a mountain barrier, habits that also spill out to the flatlands. Fewer trains mean less time spent in sidings, and if some are longer, that computes to a trade-off between tonnage and time, locomotive assignments plus other calculations. Southern Pacific expresses the solution in its own way.

Yet such is its pragmatism that *Sprint* trains flourish and continue to be established. Several city-pairs are now linked by such high-speed inter-modal runs, gliding across the landscape at express train momentum while everything else they come in contact with "takes the hole." If SP's recently well-talked-about problems are real, and not just sympathy generated for a merger proposal it's not for lack of effort or imagination.

□

This book is neither motive power roster nor historical tale. In rather loose form it attempts to portray the character of the Southern Pacific, whose personality differs considerably from that of Santa Fe, Union Pacific or Burlington Northern, carriers with which it shares the western experience. The focus is also contemporary, although there are images dating from 20 to 30 years ago.

One major difficulty has been trying to keep up with the rapid changes of late.

A case in point. Individual division maps are shown as of 1986. Immediately afterward, in early 1987, the San Joaquin Division which had been carried in a joint Los Angeles–San Joaquin Division employee timetable was eliminated, with only the L.A. designation surviving. Certain lines were cut back after the first of the year, such as the Alturas Line, whose Eugene-Ogden through freight was rerouted down the Central Valley to Roseville and over the Sierra. The typical heavy girth of the line required seven big units of helper power instead of a trio of radio-controlled types which normally worked Klamath Falls–Wendel in recent times. In the Southwest, several lightly worked branch lines in Louisiana were dumped in early 1987, and were transfigured into a new web of short lines.

Yet in spite of the changes, all the components of a working railroad remain in place, the steel rail, wooden ties, locomotives and rolling stock, which have been molded by people and physical domain into a being like no other. Although uncertainty now attends the future identity of SP, we can hope that no one pulls the pin on its great tradition.

Power assigned to the seemingly never-ending task of propping up the fill across the Great Salt Lake lines up at Lakeside, Utah, for tomorrow's assignments.

A temporary shoofly around a blocked tunnel created this scene in the desert where SP connects with the Trona Railway.

Opposite: Rolling along through northern Nevada, a CHOAT symbol is drawing a bead on the Sierra Nevada ahead.

11

Here comes the lumber from Oregon. With Klamath Falls now a couple of hours behind, a wood products freight is drifting down the flanks of Mt. Shasta.

New Year's Day, 1987, and the first good storm of the season blankets Dunsmuir, California. With very little business this particular day, the normal helper units are idle.

Opposite: Mainline action at Colfax in the Sierra. The freight in the foreground will be pulling slightly more than half its load forward. Then the helper, barely visible in the background, will bring the rear portion up to a coupling. Meanwhile, the westbound Amtrak schedule heads downhill toward the Bay Area.

Over the hump at Englewood Yard in Houston! A train-sized cut is being led out on the long lead.

A couple of yard-bound diesels idle near downtown El Paso, the backdrop for all those long trains that run from Portland to New Orleans.

14

What's this, an intermodal train in the hole just west of Lordsburg? The answer appears a few minutes later when an eastbound Amtrak schedule speeds by.

A hot July afternoon in Southern Arizona finds an eastbound train running through Dragoon as an impending thunderstorm moves in.

WHERE IT ALL BEGAN

The Sacramento Division

I F THERE IS A PLACE on this railroad where ghosts step, it is probably high in the Sierra Nevada mountains of California where an initial survey line was staked out. Today this section of roadbed is contained within a Sacramento Division map.

An extremely varied state of affairs, Sacramento Division spreads its efforts upon the flat carpet of California's Great Central Valley, then charges up and over the vast Sierra Nevada roadblock before disappearing for a few hundred miles into the depths of Nevada's expansive desert.

Destination: Ogden, Utah.

While Espee is predominantly a single-tracked railroad, the Sierra Nevada run from Roseville's ever busy yard over the airy mountaintops to Sparks, Nevada, is totally double tracked. Now that SP and UP are swapping their single tracks into a paired-track operation on the eastern section of the division, a goodly portion of the Oakland–to–Ogden run is operated with little need for sidetracking, not a typical SP norm.

At one time Sacramento Division was undoubtedly the premier story of SP railroading, but gradually emphasis has been shifted south to Los Angeles, Tucson, El Paso and on east. Not only has that area of the nation undergone significant growth, but western railroad patterns have shifted this past decade, with a long haul out of Northern California and Oregon to the south providing more revenue than handing tonnage over to Union Pacific or Rio Grande east of the Great Salt Lake.

Although each division on SP's far-flung system exhibits its own personality, none is so varied as the Sacramento. In addition to its see-saw behavior between mountain, valley and desert, it is privy to some of the heaviest snowfall in the nation. The railroad is forced, even in summer, to get ready for those moisture-laden clouds that come scudding in from the Pacific Ocean, dumping massive amounts of snow as they cross mountaintops, including those near Donner Summit where tracks are laid. The

Opposite: Lonely sentinel on the edge of the Great Salt Lake. Sunset is almost an accomplished fact at Lakeside, Utah, with just a bit of the lake showing, a territory that until a few years ago was listed separately as the Salt Lake Division but is now part of Sacramento Division's expansive limits.

17

rotary plow, the flanger, even snowplow-style pilots that grace the front end of all big units are thrown into a pitched battle starting in late fall. Nowhere else in American railroading is so much pitched into a conflict with nature's cold weather months.

Representing the northern hub of SP's California works, Roseville Yard was until the postwar development of Eugene and West Colton yards the premier West Coast facility. It has always been a major focus where north-south as well as east-west traffic has been classified, but in recent years it has assumed slightly more of an impact as the railroad has gradually pulled back from its Bay Area patterns. Places like Bayshore south of San Francisco and Oakland Yard have been downgraded a bit in favor of Roseville, which stands 105 miles inland from San Francisco's wind-whipped bay. It provides a similar stance to what has been happening over the years in Southern California, with West Colton taking over as the principal outer rim terminal.

To a large extent this move is consistent with the development of container ship traffic. Drive around the original dock areas of either San Francisco or Oakland and you won't find many ships working them. Rails leading there are rusty and there is hardly any rolling stock to be seen. As the container ship has taken over, the rail/truck terminal is more important than anything else. Once created at the piggyback-style yard, the solid TOFC/COFC train typically bypasses other yards until reaching its ultimate destination. Meanwhile, the reduced number of standard, traditional type cars are better off handled in longtime facilities such as Roseville.

Roseville's king-sized yard is split into three major segments: a receiving section which lies at its west end, the center area hump, and an east-lying departure yard. A main line skirts its northern boundary, a favorite routing for piggyback and expedited trains as they hesitate momentarily to change crews before speeding off on any of four major routings.

One of SP's pipe-laden lococomotive servicing facilities—known colloquially as "launching pads"—occupies the northeast corner of Roseville, with a major diesel engine repair shop nearby. Even when the valley is sweltering under 100 degree temperatures, a subtle reminder of winter is always present, since three or four well-painted rotary plows are parked outside the ever busy shop.

Locally the subject of foreign road motive power has become a fairly steady menu in recent years. Union Pacific yellow has been a regular visitor for some time as run-throughs traded at Ogden have carried the red and grey east, the yellow west. Following UP's incorporation of Missouri Pacific into its fold, SP has tended to get closer to its other connection at Ogden, the Rio Grande. So black-bodied diesels in orange trim by way of Denver are currently frequent visitors to Roseville, often in solid sets. It's a

Out on the Nevada desert a mixture of UP and SP power speeds a westbound toward the coast. Such combos of motive power are commonplace on this line.

more routine, sustained visitation than occurs further south where foreign road power into the Los Angeles basin takes on more of a pronounced seasonal flavor.

As Santa Fe-Southern Pacific moved toward its megamerger, rumor had it that Rio Grande would like to take over ownership of SP rail west from Ogden to just short of Roseville's yard limit sign. It might seem as hearsay to old-line SP management, but the future outlook for the overland route is one of diminishing impact.

That makes Ogden–Roseville routing a bit less significant, particularly with trains being shared with either UP or Rio Grande in the process.

Four, five, at times six, units are spliced together on some of the ready tracks at Roseville's engine complex. Next door on parallel tracks are cuts of two and three, including quite a few with four axles, not six. It's not difficult to figure which ones will slip through a maze of switch frogs and cut into a train for the "hill," and which ones will go west or south.

Classified through the hump yard's gravity flow, a car here, a long cut there, are pulled together by the perpetual motion of switchers into heavy tonnage trains to be positioned at Roseville's east end where they wait for motive power to be sent over. Solid trailer train types may shun this routine, either holding to the main or slipping through yard tracks to add "fill" before speeding out of town again.

Ogden is an outpost just like Portland's Brooklyn Yard, Avondale (New Orleans) and East St. Louis. Conclusion: There's not a great deal there, as SP's pattern is to have its major terminals inside the periphery of its system. As an example, Pine Bluff, Arkansas, brings together two important Cotton Belt links, one to East St. Louis, the other to Memphis. Inbound traffic can then be split into blocks for any of the railroad's numerous destinations, or in reverse for the many carriers that pull up to these Mississippi River connections. Eugene's central Oregon locale blends a timberland branch network with traffic out of the Northwest's major cities. Given such a pattern, it is not surprising that Ogden is somewhat of a sparse facility inasmuch as the principal business there is interchange with both UP and Rio Grande.

The basic dissimilarity with other major Espee lines is that there is no yard a hundred or so miles into the Overland Route, just a vast expanse of mostly desert followed by a short side climb of the Sierra Nevada to Roseville Yard. There's little if anything to classify at Ogden since most sorting, in or outbound, will be left to the giant California yard.

Technically, SP occupies the west end of Ogden Union Railway and Depot Company, an idea popular in railroading's past when multiple carriers combined to set up terminals, thus simplifying handover procedures. There are no switchers here bearing that name, as SP trains normally pull down through the yard for forwarding to UP. Ditto that performance on westbound moves. As for the Rio Grande, a greater relationship has been established of late. It takes place at the west end of OUR&D's web of switchstands with through movements promptly exchanged on what has become a bridge route involving both routine interchange as well as D&RGW serving as a partner in completing a span between Overland Route steel and Cotton Belt iron in Kansas.

Resulting connections find faded black Rio Grande units rocking to the curves below forested Gold Run in the Sierra while basic grey units pound their massive weight onto rail joints in Tennessee Pass.

On occasion SP will hook together a set of units, turning them over to Rio Grande in Ogden to run light to Salt Lake City's Roper Yard where they hook onto a westbound run that comes back to Espee for movement across the desert.

A train exiting Ogden toward West Coast destinations heads out into an unusual run. A few miles out the Great Salt Lake makes an appearance, its azure waters spreading into a horizon surrounded by treeless, bleak hills and mountains. Known as the Lucin Cut-off, this 24-mile-long fill carries trains to sea, in a manner of speaking, as either north or south landfall is several miles off in the vastness. Trains will cross its length at a moderate pace.

Lucin Cut-off is like Sierra mountain winter railroading on this same division, needing constant attention to keep it open, a factor in the 1980s that has never been more evident. The Great Salt Lake has been on a rising note the past few years, threatening to flood the massive fill's roadbed while requiring a year-round effort on SP's part to keep it open.

Headquarters for continual rock quarrying and fill dumping on the cut-off is Lakeside, the west end of the fill. During 1986-87, three daily work trains were kept in constant motion, shunting between loading crane and fill. This section of the railroad will often be blocked off for hours of daylight, necessitating heavier traffic at night.

Opposite: A yard-type SD-7 with 1,200-gallon tank and limited duration switches some ballast cars at the west end of Ogden Union Depot Company's yard while a long coal train off Wyoming coal fields snakes through on the main line.

21

Centered upon Lakeside, where a large crew of workers is permanently stationed, the trio of dump trains cycles from quarry out onto the strip that splits the lake. Until a couple of years ago there was no connection between north and south portions of the lake. Because of differing drainage patterns one side was 18″ or so higher than the other. Now a cut has been made in the fill, allowing waters to even out a bit, a process still going on which indicates how much volume is involved.

Outside of territory in southwest Texas and northeast New Mexico the expansive, barren Nevada desert represents some of the more sparsely settled territory this railroad sees. In today's world nothing is really remote, but little habitation occupies a few hundred miles of checkerboard landscape that geographers label the "basin and range province." The railroad picks its way through these mountains and elongated valleys on a pathway generally of fleet-footedness, but upon which there is plenty of gradient, enough in fact that in prior years a routine helper east out of Wells or west out of Ogden was not an unknown feature.

The emergence of high-horsepower motive power in second-generation form has pretty well done away with helper assignments on the desert, which, despite its image, does contain some modest grade. A heavy coal drag off UP's Wyoming Division headed for a Nevada power plant usually gets a single unit on the rear as it clears Ogden for Lucin Cut-off and the desert beyond that extra units are a rarity.

Otherwise, SP trains carve up mileposts in massive numbers. It takes but two crews to manage some 530-odd miles between Ogden and Sparks, near Reno. Assignments are broken up by either end crews running to Carlin, a mid-desert division point. As can be appreciated, there are few moments to be spent in sidetracks if engineers are to get across the division under the hours of service law. What makes it routinely possible is that mostly double track is involved.

Not the typical double track, mind you, but a longtime affiliation, first with Western Pacific, then with its follow-on, Union Pacific. For close to 200 miles' worth of rather fast curving steel the two roads share their signal indications; an SP dispatcher calls shots on westbound movements, a UP counterpart decides who holds the main and who takes siding on eastbound trains.

Actually there needs to be little waiting time on the line, because an effective double track carved from the two railroads' single-tracked lines keeps things stirring, except when an expedited freight or an Amtraker comes creeping up on a slow one. Having this centerpiece of twin tracks in the desert's heart allows a dispatcher great flexibility in scheduling moves across the area east, which is mostly single track, and the line west, which is roughly 50% double track in its own right.

This bit of Southern Pacific's widespread network displays a varied consist over the months. There are moments in January or February when

Mountains and scrub brush provide the dominant stage for Espee operations from west of Ogden to Sparks, Nevada, profiling an eastbound freight skirting the edge of a dry lakebed.

perhaps three or four moves each way are the norm, while in summer months or late fall a daily trainsheet may log a bidirectional total of 10—plus a local at one point or another, especially on the west end towards Sparks. It is also a scene where traffic seems to bunch up.

Train sounds vanish for hours at a time, desert solitude broken only by soft winds rustling through sagebrush. Then two or three hard-breathing groups of diesels come drumming along within an hour, frequently a mixed bag of SP and UP ownership in trail.

From any viewpoint there is a momentary burst of sight and sound of momentous proportions. Weaving through a tapestry of mountain to basin to mountain again are lengthy collections of trailers, boxcars and other types, taking great distance in stride as a matter of course.

In their wake silence takes over. It's like that in Nevada most days and nights as well, as fast trains go by any point in a time lapse that is measured in minutes at most.

Opposite: On paired trackage east of Carlin, Nevada, a trailer train disappears momentarily in the diesel-produced haze of making a run at one of numerous "hills" in the basin and range province; April 1985.

It takes power to move trains at speed across the basin and range province and Southern Pacific has never been one to short-change its needs in this respect. The scene is typical western desert about 20 miles east of Carlin, Nevada, April 1985.

As the Great Salt Lake has risen in recent years, SP has been forced to a constant, if expensive, response, pouring boulders and other fill into the lake on a daily basis. These Geeps are working just such a train, returning empty to Lakeside for another load of rockfill.

On heavy days Amtrak's *California Zephyr* needs an SP unit to conquer the Sierra, here shown passing through Yuba Gap.

Railroading past, railroading present. A well-preserved private observation car is tacked on the rear of Amtrak's westbound run as it heads into the early-morning shadows of the Sierra below Truckee, California.

Opposite: Among the storied names of history that line the SP's Sierra Nevada conquest is Emigrant Gap. A three-unit eastbound slides through the Gap on a wintry day while hidden from sight an additional trio of heavy-duty power is working hard on some two percent.

Running about 45 minutes ahead of the Amtrak, a westbound slips through Colfax on the double-tracked trunk that crosses the Sierra. Unless overtaken by a faster train— a not too common occurrence given train pacing—trains can run the full Sierra Nevada hill without having to take siding.

Given its many tunnels, SP has always been interested in any idea which would provide better operating techniques for its motive power. In steam days it was cab-forwards, in the diesel era it was tunnel motors with their low-lying air intakes.

Opposite: An early-morning scene at Colfax, California. A westbound freight slides downgrade with the bulk of its trip from Sparks, Nevada, now behind it.

28

THE BOXCAR RAILROAD

A look at the wooden railroad

A THROWBACK IN APPEARANCE is that part of Southern Pacific labeled the Oregon Division. Its daily menu of trains is dominated by boxcars and other styles of more traditional rolling stock upon which railroads of past decades have been so dependent. This is so because of the prevalence of wood and wood products, upon which the state of Oregon depends for its economic well-being. Complementing this scene is a maze of gathering branch lines which taps into the mountainous timber-producing regions with their on-line mills and factories, spawning locals that rarely trail anything except the standardized consist of boxcars, flats or wood chip cars. The latter is a regional peculiarity of the northwestern U.S., as well as some parts of the South where timber is also a major railroad commodity.

This is not to ignore other facets of the division's operations, for the main stem certainly offers its share of lengthy 75-foot-plus cars with their triple-decked auto racks or aluminum trailer loads. But those types of trains are now commonplace on most other SP divisions, while Oregon Division originates an uncommon tableau in the 1980s. It is where SP's brand of long trains are mobilized in Eugene Yard or along the narrow valleys to the south, with a total boxcar-flatcar mix from locomotive to caboose. This trademark is stamped upon Oregon Division so when its trains move south into other territory to blend with piggybackers and mixed movements, it's not hard to pick out those that originated up north, unless of course too much fill has been tacked on in Roseville or San Joaquin Valley terminals.

The geographic uniqueness of Oregon Division is just that, for on this widespread railroad each entity presents its own individualism, be it desert, urban sprawl or concentration upon boxcars. Although the Oregon takes in a bit of California beginning at Dunsmuir, most operations for the division are in the state for which it is named.

Opposite: Called the Boxcar Railroad by its employees, Oregon Division at Corvallis, Oregon, in midsummer 1984 shows why the nickname fits.

31

Focus momentarily now on an early weekday evening at Brooklyn Yard, a modest chunk of railroad-dedicated acreage in southeast Portland's industrial district. It represents one perimeter of Southern Pacific, the last outpost in the Northwest before running into someone else's roadbed. Like many other outlying terminals in this time of run-throughs, its importance has dropped because now some traffic, notably the hotshots, makes off-line Lake Yard in northwest Portland their sally port.

Commuters are pretty much at home at the dinner table as a four-unit set of red and grey standard bearers comes pounding into the yard from the direction of downtown Portland, its hogger engaging the distinctive whine of dynamic braking for quick deceleration. A fairly easy task, for stretched out behind is an all trailer-train configuration of girder-like flats with their rubber-tired trailers swaying on uneven rail. The CZLAT (Crown Zeller-bach-Los Angeles Trailers), as it is known, has come to fill out at Brooklyn Yard before speeding off south across a thousand miles of home rail to Los Angeles. Five, sometimes six times a week it will accomplish this routine task, originating at Burlington Northern's Lake Yard, picking up at Brooklyn Yard and possibly at Eugene to the south. Mostly, though, it is in motion.

The dispatch of this trailer train is the pressure point during a yard-master's shift, for most else is lower key in this dominion of wooden trains. Less time-urgent freights carry unclassified cars down to Eugene for humping, delivering byproducts that come off industrial sidings; they also interchange tonnage off the nearby BN and UP connections and timber products that Portland area locals pick up on the northern branches which radiate from the Rose City.

Soon CZLAT will be back in action, the yardmaster breathing easier as it clears his yard limit sign, digging in along the suburbia that flows beside the Willamette River below Portland's girth, emerging into a valley of farm and field, air horn sounding its raucous urgency upon dozens of crossings.

Los Angeles is due on the second dawn.

Brooklyn Yard is an outpost, albeit an important one in the scheme that is spun from company headquarters in San Francisco. But to really understand the dimensions of Oregon Division, Eugene Yard with its continuously clattering group of retarder gates is required reading. Easily the hub and centrally sited in the southern edge of the Willamette Valley, it brings together a radiating web of branch-line activity, injecting into the mainline happenings of the Pacific Coast's principal north-south link a trunk that connects northwest cities with population centers in California.

Activity at Eugene Yard in the mid-'80s remains pretty much as it was in the mid-'60s, although its volume has declined as Oregon's timber-related businesses have gone into a shallow dive, the industry having

The odds seem to say that Eugene's diesel tracks were temporarily short of big units, so a combination roadset with a trio of Geeps was put on the point, seen here at Wicopee Siding.

suffered from diminishing demand for wood products. From a typical 24-hour day in the mid-1970s, when a hundred or more trains were penned in on a dispatcher's sheet, the numbers have declined as mills have been closed permanently, especially the smaller ones. Furthermore, the advent of second-generation diesels with their brawnier horsepower ratings, has resulted in fewer if longer trains, as well.

Roughly a third of the way down the state from Oregon's Columbia River boundary, Eugene's busy retarder-equipped terminal sits astride the main line. To the north, Valley Line track gently rolls around to avoid a hill here or there as it approaches Portland, while southeast, close to 200 miles' worth of Cascade Line steel must first breach the rugged spinal backbone of timber-crowded mountains before speeding down the interior to Klamath Falls.

Big trains, piggybacks on their expedited schedules and even a duo of Amtrak runs operate here, contenders upon which the drama of mainline action unfolds. Yet there is much more to Eugene than splicing together heavy sections of rolled steel on either flank. The terminal is there because it supports a network of branches which provide raw materials for outward-bound heavies.

Physically, Oregon Division, whether it be a goodly portion of the main line or innumerable branch-line mileage, is dominated by timber-studded mountains. The railroad had to find its way through them by whatever means possible, so wandering roadbed, tunnels and bridgework are typical. With the notable exception of trackage in the Willamette Valley or east of the Cascades, this division is not characterized as a high-speed railroad when compared with other components like Tucson Division or Cotton Belt's Kansas City division operations.

Hardly as familiar as the Sierra Nevada to the south, the Cascade chain of mountaintop stepping-stones represents the backbone of Oregon that SP trains must routinely conquer. Threading the entire state from north to south, tree-covered slopes gaze upon the valley used by trains between Eugene and Portland. South of Eugene, however, the challenge of their existence can no longer be avoided; California can only be reached by tackling mountain grade head-on, another of the many barriers for which SP is noted.

There appear to be two ways of moving trains to the Golden State, a seemingly circuitous route by way of Klamath Falls, and a more direct route down through Roseburg and Ashland into Dunsmuir by way of Black Butte. But that is only one-dimensional map talk, for in reality, the longer way through Klamath Falls is much faster and easier. Practically all traffic moves across two principal subdivisions that link Eugene's retarder switches with Dunsmuir in Northern California. Dunsmuir is the entry to Sacramento Division rail, and to Roseville's classification yard where cars can be billed to anywhere that red and grey diesels roll.

Actually, the mileage figures for either of two routings from Northern California into Oregon, and eventually Eugene Yard, come out pretty much in a dead heat. But that is as close as they come, for they differ considerably in their surrounding environment. Routed through Klamath Falls, trains pass over a line that came into existence in the 1920s. Labeled the Cascade Line, it pretty much shuns population build-up save for the aforementioned city plus a few places near Eugene. In contrast, the original Siskiyou Line ambles through intermittent series of slopes and landforms that are mountains to some, hills to others. It does make contact with a continuing pattern of modest-sized cities and towns, places that revolve around the timber business while providing the stuff of which heavy tonnage trains are formed. Slow railroading in truth, despite its traffic sources, but the real clincher as to why it's treated as a 300-mile-long branch line in SP parlance is the existence of some 3% gradient along the mountainous Oregon-California line.

While fulfilling a very important role as an originator of carloadings, the Black Butte-to-Eugene connection is a tough one in the best of times. Slow, tortuous in the extreme, it is something to avoid. The usual once-a-day hauler south from Ashland routinely carries a four- or five-unit helper in addition to an often similar-sized road consist. At that, it is a slow, roundabout haul with each unit going flat out.

Not surprisingly, a fair portion of the line's traffic—generally north of Roseburg—finds its way north to Eugene before heading back south by way of Cascade Line movements.

For heavy duty, mountain-style railroad action, the type that is a

This is typical Siskiyou Branch territory. A turn out of Medford sorts out some wood chip cars picked up along the way. Within a half hour of this moment a through freight will be dropping down into the canyon at Glendale, Oregon, and will pick up the cars and whisk them north to Eugene to a processing plant.

Southern Pacific specialty, the drama unfolds in thick woods, along twisting steel threads and in numerous tunnel bores, and typically, in remote places, for little habitation surrounds the Cascade Sub.

Each project is a singular personality somewhat unlike the other. Each is Southern Pacific.

Eugene's busy terminal, spreading across the southern tip of Willamette Valley, collates carloadings from a dozen locals and even more timber mills and paper product plants into anyone's definition of a heavy train. From that point, California and the rest of the nation are initially all uphill. An altimeter attached anywhere locally would read a 414-foot elevation, while 98 miles to the southeast where roadbed crests the Cascade Range, it would state that 4,885 feet have been reached at appropriately named Cascade Summit.

By comparison with Tehachapi's or with Sierra Nevada's massive granite block the Cascades are slightly modest, running around 1.7% and

1.8% compared with higher numbers elsewhere on other ridge lines. Full-bodied helpers are a necessity nonetheless on boxcar trains, for predominantly wood products haulage is a heavy load under any circumstance.

Initially, the beginning miles outside Eugene are a series of mills, sawdust piles or industry related by blood line to Oregon's principal business. By slow degrees distant hills become higher on the horizon as Lookout Point Reservoir is skirted just prior to entering a narrow defile. Odds are pretty good that a helper will be cut in here, possibly at the siding at Fall Creek Jct. or at Dougren, rather than being tagged on at Eugene Yard.

There isn't much of a climb for a few miles, but at Oakridge, with its pungent odors of working wood mills, the first step begins. There will be 44 miles of heavy effort ahead now, mostly in the range of 1.5% to 1.8%, a fair couple of hours' work at least, possibly more for the heaviest moves. Train speeds are mostly limited to 30 mph over this district but that idea mainly involves descending trains.

The three units on the point of this lumber train climbing the Cascades are deceptive, for buried just out of sight around the curve is a five-unit helper.

Ever climbing, rails fall in step with Salt Creek for several miles, the two occupying a narrow bottom of a steep-walled V. Piggybacks such as CZLAT will make the ascent unaided most times, their lengthy rolling stock squealing in ear-splitting tones on numerous curves.

A dozen miles beyond Oakridge, Oregon Division's map undergoes one of SP's spectaculars. Crossing Salt Creek on a spidery-legged steel bridge, the line does a complete about face, climbing away toward the west for about six miles before reversing course again. At least momentarily, a train's timetable direction is in sync with a compass, for Eugene-Klamath Falls, while mostly following an east-to-south course, is by official designation "Westward."

Sanders working, throttles in low notches, straining SD-40s and 45s scale the basically uninhabited slopes of Umpqua National Forest in a determined run at gravity, tugging ambitious train lengths skyward. No contest with time, this is raw-boned, brute-force railroad action at its best. Noisy locomotives have slack stretched taut from stem to stern over mile-long-plus consists, with helper and caboose never in sight from foot to summit.

Some measure of what's involved is a 30-mph speed limit—an unrealized dream in a climb—on the "63 curves" between MP 537 and 553, plus a similar limit on "93 curves" covering a zone from MP 554 to 580.

Little other explanation is required.

Dense forests dampen the straining echoes of uphill trains, especially in winter when heavy snowfall at the summit on down to Oakridge makes the area virtually inaccessible except by train or snowmobile. Back in the '60s a particularly fierce winter storm took out a key bridge and otherwise made the Cascade Line inoperable for several days. While repairs were under way, regular service was detoured down the Siskiyou Subdivision complete with 3% grade, *et al.*

Cresting at Cascade Summit alongside Odell Lake, westbounds will pause. Now that the uphill battle is complete, extra power is redundant. Since most assistance is on heavy trains, odds favor a three- or four-unit mid-train profile, requiring a bit of juggling to get them out. The complete train will pull ahead so that the rear end is just past the west switch. The helper backs its portion while holding the main; it is cut off and ducks into a siding with a dispatcher throwing a power switch. The front end then backs to a coupling, makes its air-brake test and highballs on toward Klamath Falls at an accelerated pace now that the mountains have been conquered.

Meantime, the helper crew either heads back for another assignment or it ties up in Eugene. If the crew is short on hours of service, the helper will follow its former train eight miles to Crescent Lake, tie up and wait for a taxi to bring in a fresh crew or perhaps just leave the locomotive there for several hours. The current lineup will determine what happens.

The triweekly Susanville local works its way into Wendel featuring a well-worn SW-1200 up front. In early 1987 through trains were canceled on the Modoc Line leaving the likes of small power to run a local or two at either end.

In this era of fuel efficiency a major effort is geared toward not overpowering trains, though from looking at lead elements on most Espee heavyweights, that may seem a strange statement. On the fast track from Crescent Lake to Klamath Falls non-expedited trains are instructed to shut down all but three units. There are many similar such rules on Espee, particularly where a need for power varies from mountain to flat terrain to mountain again. Some diesels are equipped with a fuel-saver device as well, a concept that takes all unneeded power off-line when fairly level territory is being traversed.

Once a westbound has conquered the climb out of Eugene Yard it embarks on a rather speedy trip through high country beyond the Cascade Range's forested crests. Unless carded as an expedited train it is directed to shut down all but three units in this quite level, fast realm which is still surrounded by trees. Eastbound moves from Klamath Falls to Eugene are to follow a similar pattern as they emerge toward the Willamette Valley as are locomotives in excess of 24 axles of dynamic braking beyond Oakridge and into Eugene Yard.

In a somewhat unusual mode for Southern Pacific's system north of Sacramento, Burlington Northern has trackage rights from Chemult, Oregon, south to Klamath Falls. Green diesels thread in and out of CTC-controlled sidings over this 73-mile gap, completing the Inside Gateway between the Columbia River and Northern California by using SP's steel.

□

Among the varied operating looks provided on Oregon Division is the Modoc Subdivision out of Klamath Falls. In several ways it is one of Southern Pacific's more unusual activities, with nearly 218 miles of lightly trafficked, single-tracked line operated to either extremity without any block signals. A single lengthy train each way daily is pretty much a normal pattern; double that number is rare these days. The availability of crews, not time constraints, is what generally determines this district's scheduling. So it is not uncommon to come upon a train waiting by one of the more barren places on this railroad, Wendel, California, while an inbound crew gets enough shut-eye to qualify for a return trip to either Klamath Falls or a Sacramento Division terminal way out on the Nevada Desert.

Rationale for Modoc Sub is a connection for Eugene Yard-Ogden business where Espee connects with both Union Pacific and Rio Grande. By going down the back side of Northern California's mountain country,

Southern Pacific is a railroad with many well-known displays of artful track work. This one is lodged near Likely on the Alturas Line.

39

the railroad keeps some traffic out of Roseville Yard and off the Sierra mountaintop.

Definitely a lonely stretch of railroad, there are relatively few polished sidings as the line ambles across the Oregon-California border on a flat note, continuing on the same pattern for 80 miles to Perez where the first of several hill lines are encountered. What lies ahead means that helpers are commonly needed on Modoc Sub train movements. They too have been of a different breed in recent times, for a limited number of radio-controlled mid-train boosters have appeared here, one of the few places on the railroad where they still perform their original role.

Riding close to a 1% ruling grade beyond Perez, the line peaks at Ambrose then drops down on a short but steeper 2.0% towards Alturas where not too many years ago crews were changed. In the 1980s Alturas is just a series of whistle chords on the way to either tip of the Modoc Sub.

South of Alturas helpers earn their pay on a cross-section that resembles a roller coaster. They come in very handy now on 7,000-ton-plus trains as they slowly push through a horseshoe-style curve near Likely while scaling a ladder towards a 5,500-foot summit at Sage Hen. Quickly appearing is another downhill sequence as the lead units shift into a whining regenerative mode. In quick succession there is a level slab, then more ups and downs that run to 1.7%–1.9% and, ultimately, a modest group of weatherbeaten buildings on the fringes of Nevada's expansive desert.

Wendel is unlike any of SP's present-day division points. Bordered by bleak hills to the north, its south side stretches away to a dry lake with the great Sierra Nevada chain towering above its western flank. Off eastward, twin ribbons of processed iron ore disappear into a limitless horizon. Winds blow more often than not, bone chilling in winter turning into a steady diet of hot dust in summer.

Coming out of Eugene Yard by way of Klamath Falls the basically wood-heavy trains are geared to a slow pace, routinely cooling their wheels at Wendel while waiting for a Sacramento Division crew to become legally available for train service. Subdivision steel extends some 20-odd miles on east where trackage rights over Union Pacific are used as a shortcut to home rails out on Nevada's arid spaces.

Mostly empties move back into Oregon, and nowhere on Oregon Division's home rails is the boxcar image more obvious, since few piggyback or auto rack waybills travel this way in either direction.

A hundred or so miles west across numerous mountain peaks is a 300-mile line which is totally block signaled throughout but carded officially as a branch line. The Siskiyou Subdivision was until the mid-1920s the sole way to move from California to Oregon. In today's scene its 40-mph guiding speed limit boards extend from stem to stern, hardly the sort of roadbed for competitive running. As with other elements of Oregon Division it presents its own brand of individualism. On its south

40

Bearing the most recent servicing marks on its cab sides . . . RV MOO 6-83 . . . a venerable SD unit idles through the early hours of a July 1983 night at Dunsmuir. The engine shed in the background now houses only M of W paraphernalia, not idling diesels.

end it provides little originating traffic, but once north of the Siskiyou Mountain chain and into Oregon it becomes a heavy originator. A slow railroad to run, the Siskiyou Sub geographically occupies center stage below Eugene while providing more mountainous ups and downs than anywhere on this widespread division. It also has within its bounds the heaviest mainline gradient on SP, several miles' worth of 3.3% and a bit of 3.7% to a crest on the Oregon-California state line. Although designated a branch, any observance of action here justifies calling it a main stem.

Glancing at a map the Siskiyou route seems roughly as long as the Cascade line via Klamath Falls. Going north, the two lines separate at Black Butte, California, coming back together just shy of Eugene Yard. As for mileage, both are almost in a dead heat, but the map appraisal is only a one-dimensional standard since when you add a second, a profile, a difference in operating characteristics is measurably unlike.

A lot of carloadings are generated in southern Oregon on the Siskiyou Line, although because of its difficult physical characteristics many of them take a quite circuitous route north into Eugene Yard where they are assembled into trains for movement over the Cascade Subdivision. Grants Pass is normally the boundary, everything to the south moving through Ashland.

Dunsmuir daily originates a northbound run to Ashland; ditto from that point the other way. Both trains often use Black Butte, a narrow yard

Dunsmuir, California, early in the second-generation scheme and without the bold "S.P." on the nose. An Alco Century leads a train uphill past an idling SD-40.

up the hill from Dunsmuir to work their consists. Given a dominance of forest products hereabouts, the heavy moves come south into Dunsmuir while empties fill out reverse moves. And what moves they are! Nowhere else on Southern Pacific will such a formidable gauntlet be thrown up to challenge red-nosed units.

Often, a fairly light train is dispatched uphill out of Dunsmuir, picking up more cars and helpers at Black Butte, the junction where Siskiyou and Black Butte Subdivisions part company. Nearby Mt. Shasta dominates a local skyline at this point where the railroad intermittently stables a few helpers to be used on both subs. The yard here is narrow, inclined toward the south with all but Ashland-bound trains and a local or two generally skirting it. In recent years places like Dunsmuir have lost some of their usefulness as most classifying is done in the principal terminals. Consequently, some tracks there have been ripped out leaving Black Butte available for local needs.

A prominent, almost perfectly formed black cinder cone of the same name casts its shadow over Black Butte, a junction splitting Siskiyou and Black Butte Subdivisions from one another to the north. Trains speed by on their way to Klamath Falls taking a brief respite on flat ground before climbing toward Grass Lake, a route that the bulk of trains will take.

The relatively few Siskiyou Sub moves head-in over approach switches, then they begin a series of introductory curves, jogging on a

42

descent that extends for eight miles into Shasta Valley's lower end. Most of the descent runs close to 2% but a half mile of 3% really makes loaded trains out of Ashland grunt and groan as they reach for the junction.

Nor is this uncommon, since you can count the number of level mileposts between here and Eugene on two hands and feet.

Shasta Valley is host for the roadbed to just short of Hornbrook, although it is hardly smooth, as tracks tilt down to Montague then immediately reach uphill, then down, then upward again. It becomes a regimen that overshadows the entire subdivision from Black Butte to just shy of Eugene's retarder yard.

North of Hornbrook, SP takes up with a mountain pass unrivaled in U.S. railroading. As track disappears into a stand of Douglas firs, the zigzag approach to a summit encounters five miles of line, including a healthy chunk of 3%. That plus a similarly sized gradient on the Ashland side has

Looking a bit overpowered the Weed Turn of another era grinds uphill towards the junction at Black Butte.

43

relegated this subdivision to secondary status despite its position as a tonnage originator.

Another unusual holdover here is an occasional stand of semaphore signals, something hardly ever seen elsewhere on the system, except at a few spots east of Tucson.

This would be a helluva railroad to run with any kind of density at all, its steep see-saw pattern alternating between brute strength in a climb or equal forces held at bay in a descent. Abundantly clear is that full-length trains are a tough breed to move from point to point on the Siskiyou. Thus their relative scarcity is limited to whatever the territory produces. Through cars are kept off as much as possible, with additional restrictions on especially long cars.

A maximum horsepower-to-ton ratio of 3.0 is fairly standard over much of SP, while from Ashland to Roseburg that limit is extended to 4.0. But for all trains between Black Butte and Ashland it is way up, 6.0, similar to that governing eastward trains over Tehachapi.

From its crest, the north side of Siskiyou Pass is 13 miles' worth of tobogganing toward Ashland, the least of which is a two-mile-long segment of 2%, while the bulk varies between 2.7% and 3.1%. No wonder loaded trains run to 10 units of six-axled marks.

Either way, sand spills under screeching flanges as several thousand tons of train line claw laboriously uphill, or five units wail in protest on the opposite slope, demonstrating that this is one difficult railroad.

The story of Siskiyou Subdivision is one of yard limits.

Most of its basic commodity list, wood and wood products, is picked up from a wide variety of origins. On this major beam in SP's framework local turns bring their loads to gathering points for pickup, coincidentally dropping off empties for tomorrow's loads.

The Roseburg Turn, for example, which goes on duty at that city, runs north to Glendale. The 65-mile haul takes six or seven hours, what with making business calls at several lumber mills. Called on duty in midmorning, it scoots out of town behind a trio of rebuilt SD9s, a common type of motive power hereabouts, one well suited for local service. Initially, a dozen or so empties, a mixture of flats and boxcars, trails behind, but by the time rural Glendale is encountered, 20 or so loads, including several wood chip cars, will be in the consist.

Wood chip cars are a rarity throughout much of the system, but in Oregon they prove to be a commonplace item in many trains.

Though only a "turn" of local proportions, the roadbed ahead is a topsy-turvy pace typical of this district, at times forcing the SD9s into a low-speed, heavy-breathing activity more typical of a heavy tonnage drag. Two major grades with a low point midway stand between Roseburg and Glendale.

Upon reaching Glendale the local begins performing switching chores on a trio of tracks' worth of wood chip empties. A few minutes later, a four-unit set of SD45s hauling a Eugene-bound through movement comes charging into town, stopping quickly behind a heavy application of brakes, its motors strapped into regenerative off the last hill. Pausing a few minutes it picks up the loads provided by the Roseburg Turn then saunters off at a fairly leisurely gait and enters one of the railroad's more understated spectaculars, Cow Creek Canyon.

In terms of recognition, Cow Creek Canyon isn't the Sierra nor Cajon Pass. And while its daily train sheet isn't one with many markings, it is nevertheless one more link in this railroad's exceptional western panorama.

Pushing through a narrow slit in Oregon's coastal ranges, Cow Creek Canyon spins away from all but the barest of habitation till track spills out into yet another verdant valley, often hazy in scented smoke from a clutch of sawmills. During winter's lengthy weeks drizzle and rain create an atmosphere that is rare beyond northwest states.

□

So goes Siskiyou: a part of Espee that dwells in turns, locals, through trains of a fashion, and the timber business, but never with any particular urgency, for this is a 300-mile-long branch, a blend of big cuts of heavyweight locomotives guided by such things as semaphore signals, with many upthrusts to subdue.

There is nothing like it on Southern Pacific. But then, this railroad is a compilation of just such statements.

Black Butte, Calif., a railroad junction so named for the obvious geological feature in the background, is where the Siskiyou Line and Klamath Falls Line split or merge depending upon direction. Both routes play host to helper sets running up to four and five units.

The impact of a telephoto lens puts an entire train into the perspective of Mt. Shasta on a summer day as a Siskiyou Line train plods its way toward the outside world with its heavy carloads of Oregon timber products.

The daily Siskiyou Line train curves through Weed, California, with a train comprised mostly of empties returning to the lumber mill sidings of southern Oregon.

Late last night this all-trailer train was highballed out of Eugene Yard. Now it's early morning the next day and the train is coming down the mountainside into Black Butte, California, December 1984.

Well-traveled 9333 is waiting at Dunsmuir, assigned today at least to helper duty.

48

Opposite: A through train each day plus a yard goat that doubles as power on the Susanville local is all that keeps Wendel in business on the lightly trafficked Alturas Line, the shortcut from central Oregon to Ogden, Utah.

The 8351 came south out of Klamath Falls as a remote helper on the Modoc Line the day before. Now it's going back as the lead unit on the head end out of Wendel, California. This scene would shortly end, for about 10 days after this late December 1986 photo the Modoc Line was shorn of through freights, left only with an occasional local.

About two weeks after this late December 1986 photo was taken, the Modoc Line's through status was downgraded to local only business. The lighted hot box indicator was an endangered species as well, as SP made the transition to the "talker type" on most of its mainline roadbed.

Rolling through a series of curves below Oakridge, Oregon, the southbound *Shasta Daylight* appears toward the end of its career in 1969.

Though it is technically known as a branch line, the entire district between Black Butte and Eugene by way of the Siskiyous is protected by block signals. Because it is slow, mountainous and curvy most of the way, some fairly old systems can be found north of Medford, one of the few areas on the SP to still display semaphore blades.

Opposite: Twilight has settled over Oakridge, Oregon, in this scene, a bit unusual for the usually heavy-unit cuts of SP power. Only two tunnel motors are seen on the head end.

BAYWATCH

San Francisco and the Coast Route

O F ALL MAJOR WEST COAST ports none has a greater natural beauty than San Francisco. The Bay Area—a description that extends south to San Jose and across inland waters to Oakland and Richmond—has long been a major player in Southern Pacific's rail empire. Corporate-wise, it is the HQ, the place where ambitious, career-minded people have desired to be. After all, this is where decisions on how to run a railroad are made.

One Market Plaza, San Francisco, California, has not been especially jubilant recently. The railroad never seemed to recover from the last recession, financial pressures have continued and even a hint of bankruptcy has been floated. It has been very much like the Bay Area's bustling rail yards, for they too have been on a downhill slide of late, their place in the sun dimmed. Changing traffic patterns, economics of land use, technology, and other doctrines have fused in an accelerated pattern to shake up a traditional way of directing trains.

Commuter trains no longer ply their daily trade in grey flannel, having given that up for a modernistic clutch of colors devised by some artist(?) employed by a state agency called Caltrans. West Oakland's diesel shop was closed as part of a cost-cutting move in 1985, much of its responsibility shifted to Roseville.

As merchandise trailers and containers gradually take over the rail scene, the old, flat switching yards lose their importance, along with an inescapable fact that land in proximity to city centers is worth far more as commercial development than as switching territory. Industrial sidings that connect warehouses, etc., are passe anyway, their former business now geared to piggyback ramps at a central location. Just as Los Angeles' Taylor Yard has been shuttered, with duties shifted to West Colton on the fringe of the basin, so the prime Bay Area freight yard, West Oakland, is undergoing a downgrade, some of its marshaling chores shifted to other yards, notably Roseville's hump.

Opposite: A weekend finds one of the commuter-assigned SDP-45s, the 3209, heading up a westbound freight skirting along the upper reaches of San Francisco Bay near Martinez, California. A train bound for Roseville uses the other part of this double-tracked main.

53

As SP turned over its commute business to Caltrans, locomotives formerly dedicated to shuffling between downtown San Francisco and San Jose were released to work in freight service, not a totally new idea. During the past 15 to 20 years the commute units usually did weekend duty pulling their weight in freight service. Saturday night might find an SDP-45 being refueled at Taylor Yard's diesel shop, having come south on a freight from Bayshore Yard or San Jose. At that very moment another of the 3200 class would be muttering in heavy voice through Gold Run in the Sierra, putting in time as part of a helper set. Meantime the passenger geared GP-9s would be working the Valley, teamed with other small units on a turn out of Stockton, or waiting for a highball from a Fresno Yard departure track.

Come Monday morning, they would be lined up by San Jose roundhouse, fueled and ready for another week in first class service.

Today the former commute units are pretty well scattered throughout the system, just part of the freight pool. Recently, two GP40P-2s were seen working a drag east out of San Antonio, tying up overnight in the shadow of Flatonia's wooden tower before heading back the next morning. They had gone from the pinnacle of first-class travel to a grubby existence of being put in the hole for every opposing movement. The larger units will be used that way, smaller types, the GP-9s will undoubtedly run out their remaining life as yard goats, or on local trains.

Looking back a few years, one notes the general demise of San Francisco as a destination for freight trains. Much oceangoing traffic has shifted across the bay to Oakland as containers have become the principal activity for large ships. Very few boats, hardly ever a boxcar, are seen at the docks anymore. Bayshore Yard south of town is for all practical purposes gone and the industrial south side displays all sorts of tracks that are simply rusting, now that former boxcar loads are shifted to piggyback crane instead of plant side rail. As the process continues so do demands for switching crews in favor of trailer/container terminals.

Watching SP experiment, test, change its mind about motive power lashups has always been an intriguing subject. During the mid-'70s Bayshore's yard and engine terminal spawned a standard blend of large and small power on transbay runs, trains that worked their way over to West Oakland and back, or sometimes to Roseville.

By straight line it is just a few miles from Bayshore to West Oakland. By train, down the Peninsula and up the suburb-lined East Bay, it measures over 60 miles. During the time period in question a pattern emerged, calling for an SD-45 or 40 on the point, a four-motored GP-9 trailing. Then, the SF drawbridge was active, while today any rail moves between the two major Bay cities must travel an even further distance, going by way of a junction just north of San Jose.

San Francisco to San Jose, the Peninsula. Oakland to San Jose, the East Bay. These are the terms of local railroading.

Oakland Terminal's engine servicing tracks play host to a couple of SW-1500s between terminal assignments. BART runs nearby in the background.

Crowded with suburbia and sprawling with industry large and small, the Bay Area is forced into a somewhat narrow base by coastal mountains on both sides. On the San Francisco side they stand between the railroad and Pacific Ocean waters. In the East Bay they cause SP to reach out the south end or to follow a wide river gap that flows to the state's interior. The bulk of SP train action takes place among the East Bay cities.

Reduced in stature in the '80s, West Oakland still provides the Bay Area with its single most prolific terminal. The diesel shop may be dark, yet there is still a heavy schedule of road units in town needing refueling, sand or other expendables. Fringed by auto rack tracks and trailer/container resources, West Oakland Terminal sprawls in semicircle fashion around the ever busy port region. Towering ship cranes, ramps for imported automobiles cluster densely at the yard's periphery. Like most modern ports, Oakland appears nothing so much as a giant parking lot for stacks of brightly colored containers and new cars.

Southern Pacific loves it!

Who's working the railroad? This lineup of motive power at Oakland's busy terminal suggests a scarcity of trains at the moment, but it's merely an ebb in the busy flow of Bay Area traffic.

Logically the area moves to a rhythmic beat of switch engines toiling leads, locals arriving from nearby towns and the occasional drumbeat of a heavy freight off the Sierra held out of the yard temporarily so a Portland-bound trailer train can hit the main running.

Principal links for Bay Area moves are with Los Angeles (Coast Route), Roseville (Overland Route), Eugene-Portland (the Northwest), Tracy-Fresno-West Colton (Valley and Sunset-Golden States Routes) along with anywhere in between. Coastwise there has always existed an important hub, the Bay Area communities of Oakland and San Francisco, with San Jose serving as the split. As steam became first-generation diesel, Southern Pacific continued on with its overnight hotshots, the Coast Merchandisers east and west, a freight train counterpart of the *Daylight* streamliner between north and south. Originating as a solid clan of specialized, high-speed boxcars with a distinctive logo, these swift night runners quickly became trailer trains hammering across 460 miles of Coast

56

Line behind Fs, Geeps and eventually the 3,000-plus horsepower breed that now crowd a roster.

Today, as an early morning sun rises red on West Oakland or Los Angeles' widespread intermodal terminal, train sheets record the arrival of an LAOAC (Los Angeles-Oakland Containers) or an OALAT (Oakland-Los Angeles Trailers) braking to a conclusion at opposite ends, a routine though demanding trip now past tense.

An SP train is often more than a single symbol. Rarely either solid piggyback or solid containers, the computer friendly jargon of train identity would take a mixed bag of both types of modern equipment so that an LAOAC and an LAOAT would be a single schedule. Alternately, should a train be mostly trailers with few containers it would probably go out with the "T" designation only. General exceptions to this mixed set of metaphors would be "pure" runs such as those for ocean shippers, with their head to tail silhouette of double-stack container cars, or general freight trains such as a EULAY which move from terminal to terminal with whatever is headed in that direction.

Aluminum boxed traffic, whether on wheels or not, is also a big item between West Oakland and the Northwest. Although not an overnight guarantee, the trip is half again as long as that to Southern California, with its mountain barricades eating into the average. Following its late evening departure, an OABRT (Oakland-Brooklyn, Oregon) trailer train will be winding cautiously through the Sacramento River Canyon close to Dunsmuir by midmorning, carded to be unloaded in Portland's east side yard some time after midnight. Included in its cars may be some that originated in Los Angeles. Usually Bay Area-Northwest expedited trains will be routed by way of Davis and the so-called West Valley Line which runs its straight course toward Red Bluff by way of Willows, joining the more heavily used Dunsmuir-Roseville course at Tehama. Depending upon need, EULAY's (Eugene, Oregon, to West Colton, California) haulers may be routed through West Oakland and down the coast by way of Los Angeles, rather than across the Valley floor to Bakersfield and the mountain district that lies beyond. A somewhat circuitous routing for nonexpedited trains in both directions, it serves to keep them away from faster, more important traffic when crowded conditions prevail.

With its yard limits boards pressing on San Francisco Bay, West Oakland's role as a terminus for the Overland Route is perhaps its most celebrated. Now that Union Pacific is a direct competitor for port carloads, SP is not quite as enthusiastic about the Ogden Gateway, the Overland's eastern flank where trains are exchanged with UP. More business now is handed over to Rio Grande's black and orange fraternity at Ogden, one result being that many westbound trips carry D&RGW units west to Roseville, even into West Oakland. Rio Grande is also a "bridge" for selected Espee trains, hooking Overland Route steel with Golden State roadbed at

Herington, Kansas, an even deal made possible by the MP-UP merger which brought D&RGW rights into Kansas City. Where time is a consideration in obtaining business, the use of Rio Grande over the Rockies is certainly beneficial. Otherwise, SP prefers the long haul by way of Arizona and New Mexico and the revenue that goes with it.

Typically, high-priority trains, along with trailers, containers and auto racks will be blocked at West Oakland, staying on mainline rail through Roseville, run around congestion and pausing only for a crew change, with perhaps a helper added. Other, more traditional freights will be loosely collected at Bay Area points, allowed to enter the yard at Roseville for classification.

On this sprawling railroad, which encounters such a wide spectrum of operations more or less dictated by geography, Western Division's control of Bay region action extends over yet another different feature, the 87-mile-long Martinez Subdivision, joining West Oakland and Sacramento with Roseville's mighty yard complex. The background setting is double track spanning the entire subdivision, a facet uncommon to SP outside of Northern California. Each of the road's major double-track segments: the commute zone, San Francisco to San Jose; the Sierras, Roseville-Sparks; and the West Oakland-Roseville stretch, are local to this region. One might include Nevada desert ops but keep in mind that it realistically involves two carriers, SP and UP, making do with one directional flow on essentially two single tracks. Bits and pieces of double track exist elsewhere, generally without the same impact that Northern California exhibits.

Southern Pacific functioning under double-track rules is primarily a California idiosyncrasy. Two unambiguous rules influence the existence of Martinez Sub, D-97 and D-251. The first states: "When authorized by timetable, trains moving with the current of traffic may run extra without train order authority." The next is quoted as follows: "On portions of the railroad on designated tracks as specified in the timetable, trains will run with reference to other trains in the same direction by block signals whose indications will supersede the superiority of trains." The same pair appears as guidelines wherever the system contains a cross-section of double track, which outside of Northern California isn't much.

The luxury of running trains without meeting opposition has never been much of a Southern Pacific trademark.

As freights slip out the north end of West Oakland's curved complex they are joined by a flurry of passenger schedules that is second only to the commuter list displayed at Third and Townsend Street station in downtown San Francisco. Not really that big, it is an exclusively Amtrak act. The list includes two from the Los Angeles-Portland service, two off the Overland, plus four on San Joaquin Valley duty between Oakland and Bakersfield, providing Western Division timetables with an old-time flavor, even if trains are actually run for a government-sponsored agency. On the West

Weeds, broken windows and an ancient SP logo mark the roundhouse at San Jose which despite its appearance was still in use in 1983, providing overnight service to the likes of an SDP-45 approaching the end of its brief assignment.

Coast only Los Angeles to San Diego provides heavier Amtrak service. San Joaquin Valley service uses a combination of SP-Santa Fe roadbed, Oakland to Port Chicago on Martinez Sub, the rest of the way to Bakersfield via AT&SF.

The populous Bay Area is very evident as Southern Pacific's twin tracks spill northward out of Oakland, plunging through city after city, mile upon mile, a conflicting potpourri created from main line with extensive yard limits extending throughout. Petroleum refineries, varied industrial settings generate a mix of block signal territory, yard limits for 33 miles outside West Oakland to Bahia where finally twin ribbons get clear, flowing now in the open, as much as is possible in the nation's most populated state. The line of march which departed Oakland on a generally arctic heading turns inland past Richmond, curving to parallel the widening mouth of the Sacramento River delta as it flows through Carquinez Strait. For more than a dozen miles, SP tracks wander along a water level course, slipping below steep dirt cliffs in easy fashion to Martinez, where paths part. Double track crosses the strait on a spectacular steel bridge for Sacramento; the Mococo Line stays on the south bank, quickly becomes commonplace single track and heads for Tracy. The lesser known *San Joaquin Daylight* utilized this routing on its Oakland-Los Angeles run in other years.

Once across the bridge, roadbed straightens out on an angle toward Sacramento, the West Valley Line departing for Northern California and

Oregon at Davis, a longtime college town, once a very busy place when multiple passenger trains sped between Sacramento and Oakland. Davis serves Amtrak, as well as providing a connection to the north, a bypass of sorts for hotshots, keeping them out of Roseville Yard should a dispatcher so opt. On a regular basis the expedited trailer trains between Bay Area terminals and the Northwest tread this way. At Suisun-Fairfield, located between Bahia and Davis, a junction provides access to the Northwestern Pacific Railroad that is listed under its own heading, though an outside observer would only see SP.

Until recently Schellville to Eureka was a 243-mile-long operation, but NWP sold a major portion of its track, north of Willits, to the shipper-owned Eureka Southern. The parent got rather tired of maintaining it over the years. Its primary route lies along the Eel River, a water course which seems to go on a rampage every few years, lying as it does on the west coastal edge of northwest California. Reduced to about a 100-mile main stem between Schellville and Willits, NWP is reached by way of a 24-mile-long district of unsignaled roadbed that leaves off at Susian-Fairfield with connections to Roseville. Portions of branch yard around Santa Rosa are still mapped under the heading Petaluma and Santa Rosa Railroad Company, an ex-juice operation that SP put in its catalog decades ago.

□

South—east by timetable—out of West Oakland is the rarely overworked single-track line followed by Coast Line trains. Immediately beyond the yard, track splits the pavement of Jack London Square, a tourist site developed by Oakland where auto and pedestrian traffic mix it up with grey diesels toting long strings of rolling stock. A pair of separate single tracks course south to San Jose allowing a choice. At San Jose they meet the commute line down from San Francisco. The one-time Tracy Line, which went from Redwood Jct. on the Peninsula across the aging San Francisco drawbridge and on to Tracy by way of Altamont Pass, crossed the twin lines out of Oakland, its most publicized attribute being Niles Tower, recently axed. The whole line over the pass is gone, SP using the UP main through the hills when necessary, which isn't often.

Between northwest cities and Southern California or eastern points the Coast Line occupies a less-than-preferred position. Such reasoning is not difficult to understand. First of all, the Coast lies a bit west of San Joaquin Valley rail, resulting in a somewhat roundabout right-of-way. Over the years SP has never pumped in a lot of capital improvements, either. No CTC exists other than a local installation over bothersome Cuesta grade, and a tiny amount at Watsonville Jct. Nor are siding lengths compatible with present-day train size, at least on Espee. The average distance between siding switches in San Joaquin Valley CTC territory—in other words, the entire area—is 8,300–8,500 feet; on the Coast, around 4,700–5,000. The 7,000–8,000-foot freights that SP runs so casually are

Opposite: Long the stomping grounds of SD-9s, the Northwestern Pacific exists to bring lumber from the northwest coast of California to the outside world.

61

hard put to encounter one another so conveniently under these limitations. The alternative is of course to run fewer trains, taking care to meet them at a few selected locales with the longer sidings, or to use an alternate portion of the railroad.

Someday the Coast might become a favored alley for Sprint-style trains, short, solid strings of high-speed intermodal traffic with reduced crews. For now, that's merely conjecture, a potential.

South of San Jose, past the peripheral influence of San Francisco, extends a lengthy single track, a profile that continues to Southern California. There is some agriculture along the way. The Salinas Valley, the Santa Maria Valley are two such sources of refrigerator cars in both past and present, but there is not much else to any degree known in the Great Central Valley. During spring and summer two sugar plants, one near Salinas, another near Santa Maria, attract large cuts of cars, sometimes entire trains, to their refining processes. Imperial Valley sidings are a major origin, a solid sugar beet move entrained in old wooden, high-sided cars, heavy of foot and driven up Beaumont Pass to the accompaniment of a lot of power including mid-train helpers. Passing through Los Angeles' ever busy terminal operations, they pose a throwback look on the Coast Line when passed by a haughty, trendy set of aluminum trailers on their fashionable wheels. Other beet cars move out of the San Joaquin Valley, working slowly up through Tracy to West Oakland and then south.

"Coast Line" implies a geographic endorsement of the Pacific Ocean on a long-term basis, an idea that is merely half truth. SP doesn't come within clear line of sight of the vast sea until well south of San Jose, whereupon it skips through a narrow defile in coastal mountains to Watsonville Jct. A branch leads back north along the beach from this division point, while for a few miles only water is visible from the main line arcing south, though it quickly turns inland, coming back to a beach below San Luis Obispo at Pismo Beach, more than 150 miles farther. Roadbed takes shape much of this time along the line of the Salinas River, a narrow valley between two rows of coastal mountains, keeping them on either side of a locomotive to Santa Margarita, the Coast's choke point. Cuesta grade now looms abruptly as a short but necessary pause for attaching air hoses to a helper engine.

The typical drag may lay over in San Luis Obispo for an hour or so before continuing on. Often it waits for a local working Guadalupe, and the Santa Maria Valley Railroad connection, or other places to clear before setting forth towards Los Angeles.

The ocean, as in "Coast," becomes part of an SP poster for real south of the division point, a basically midway terminal of modest proportions as well as an encounter between Western Division and Los Angeles Division territorial rights.

After passing through Pismo Beach, with its vivid sand dunes, the line plays a bit of hide and seek with Pacific Ocean till just north of Vandenburg Air Force Base. From that spot to Ventura a good hundred miles of the railroad never puts an engineer out of sight of water. It is what one imagines a coastline operation should be.

With Los Angeles Division iron underfoot south of San Luis Obispo the path will eventually turn east below Ventura, specifically at Oxnard. Following a valley or so, it ultimately skips through another of many coastal ranges, burrowing along in a long tunnel into that sprawling metropolis, Los Angeles.

There will be days, particularly in midyear, when the Coast's reputation as a moderately busy railroad will be tested. A sugar beet train edging north through spray-crusted sidings, an unexpected EULAY working the scenic course from Oakland, perhaps a solid movement of lithe container cars taking the land bridge away east will be breaking into movement, wheels still hot from a burning descent of Cuesta. Possibly only a single set of helpers is momentarily available at San Luis Obispo this particular day, a normal circumstance for that usually low-key division point.

Decisions! Decisions!

In terms of age, Amtrak's presence is a microsecond on the earth's surface when compared with the sedimentary strata revealed at low tide on the coast south of Gaviota.

North of Gaviota a freight rumbles across a steel bridge with the Pacific Ocean hazily apparent behind.

The Spanish-style motif of SP's Santa Barbara station already has an Amtrak sign attached in the mid-'70s as the northbound coast passenger train brakes to a stop behind a pair of SDP-45s.

Opposite: During the mid-'60s, Espee experimented with four-motored U25Bs on many of its lines, including the Los Angeles–San Francisco run. Here is a quartet of U25s featuring the lead unit of the class—7500—on the point south of Watson-ville Jct.

PASSING OF AN INSTITUTION

The Bay Area commuter trains

ENTHUSIASTS OF SAN FRANCISCO have long maintained the city has the look, the dignity, perhaps a formality associated with an eastern metropolis.

Opinions aside, what "The City"—a haughty nickname intended to confer an inferiority complex upon larger Los Angeles—does have that is totally unique on the western scene is commuter trains.

Now that the region has joined every other commuter district in the U.S. by having the government run and subsidize service, Southern Pacific no longer endures the barbs of attempting to satisfy the typically hard-to-please commute crowd. Given the railroad's longtime history of not being overly enthusiastic about passenger service, this is a recent plus, one of the few of late.

As bright colors created by Caltrans replace the conservative grey tones of rolling stock, few tears will be shed in company offices. During the years following World War II, SP, like most railroads, displayed a decided interest in becoming a freight-only institution, which is precisely what occurred. In contrast, as suburbs flourished on the Peninsula south of the city, the commuter train gained in stature. But not initially, for the building of freeways at first seemed to diminish a need for mass transportation, to be followed by a rediscovery of its efficiency as the term "gridlock" entered dictionary form.

The diesel years of Southern Pacific's commuter railroad created a degree of interest for train-watchers far beyond its physical scope. Admittedly unusual to the western rail scene, ops featured specimens of motive power and rolling stock that in themselves had few peers.

Two types of equipment, one a locomotive, the other a passenger car, provided Bay Area passenger service its claim to publicity. As the 1970s arrived, a 16-unit class of Fairbanks-Morse H-24-66 Trainmasters was still faithfully handling the bulk of daily assignments. F-M had long since

Opposite: Racing homeward with a full train's worth of suburbanites, a single Trainmaster hews to a tight schedule with a mixed brand of Harrimans and gallery cars.

67

One of the afternoon out-bound fleet speeds through the area made famous by baseball's Candlestick Park.

departed locomotive building and elsewhere in the nation its products were considered antique. Yet on SP a daily, busy ritual of passenger service continued as it had for over 15 years. Pulled behind many of the FM's daily exertions was an even older example of the carbuilder's craft, 1920s-designed "Harriman Cars," with their rounded roof and protruding air vents. Riders called them "subs" for suburban, but more frequently complained about their age, riding qualities and general appearance.

Not wanting to invest heavily in a part of the business whose profit potential was marginal at very best, yet tiring of the negative publicity associated with its commuter district, SP ultimately ordered three classes of gallery cars to replace and supplement the subs. By eastern standards it wasn't much, 10 galleries from Pullman Standard in 1955, another 30 from American Car and Foundry in 1957 and, finally, 15 more from Pullman in 1968. There were enough on hand so that, except during peak periods, most Harrimans not yet scrapped were idled. Still a few soldiered on till 1986 when the arrival of new rolling stock put PAID to their 60-year service career.

The sixteen 190-ton F-M hi-noses couldn't handle the commute trains by themselves, and so required the long-term addition of 11 GP-9 units numbered 3000–3010. Equipped with dual cab controls, they usually operated in pairs. With Amtrak's birth and SP's dropping of passenger service on its own account, the 3200–3209 class of SDP-45s were transferred to San Francisco commuter traffic, replacing the faithful Trainmasters, which by the mid-'70s, were among the road's oldest group of road power. The last diesels ordered for commuter duty were a few GP-40P-2s, thereby

68

finishing off the investment in the late '70s. Two SD-9s, the 4450 and 4451, also appeared on a regular basis down the Peninsula with gallery cars and their ancient companions, the subs.

On weekends, SP made good use of what for the railroad were narrowly based engines. Not so much the FMs, when they existed, but the EMD power got into a lot of freight hauling. Down the coast to Los Angeles, east to Sparks, or on other assignments within a 300–400 mile radius. Monday morning they had to be backturned out of the San Jose roundhouse or a facility near the Third and Townsend suburban station in the "City." They couldn't be wandering afield with a freight train.

With the arrival of Caltrans and the state's purse things have changed. New passenger cars, new motive power.

A casual observer of Bay Area commuter service would have seen little to differentiate a commuter train of 1965 from that of 1985. At the end SP had hardly changed. There were no Trainmasters stuttering along its track, but just about everything else was as it had been for a quarter century, in look and in atmosphere. Gallery cars, themselves high-time rolling stock, were occasionally mixed with a few absolutely ancient "subs"; a white SP was emblazoned on diesel noses, and platforms were lined with people reading newspapers, looking quite bored about the whole thing.

The past, present and future were one.

Not, however, as Southern Pacific.

Banking sharply, a train made up of ancient but serviceable Harriman cars leaves downtown San Francisco for its afternoon run to San Jose.

It's midday in downtown San Francisco and about the only thing actively working are the switchers, a typical commuter operation pattern which takes place "in between."

Tender—perhaps not loving—care kept the Trainmasters going for years past their expected demise, an opportunity represented by the fact that they never wandered far from home base and every night were available for servicing.

In keeping with the traditions of commuter service around the nation an off-peak hours train is light enough to be handled by a single low-horsepower unit as it emerges from a tunnel near Bayshore.

In anticipation of Cal Train's eventual takeover, some gallery cars were painted ahead of the eventual arrival of their own power, mixing with SP power that would be released to freight service in the months ahead.

POWER
ON THE HILL

Tunnels, mountains and big diesels

O F ALL THE VARIED components that work to build a railroad's personality a unique feature associated with Southern Pacific would have to be the employment of helper power on its western lines. There is no railroad in the United States that crosses more mountains, assaults more gradient, winds around so many curves, or has as many tunnels, as Espee.

This makes the western-based railroad the largest user of extra power on typical train movements in this land.

A geologist cataloging western railroads could not help but come to an obvious conclusion, namely, there is no more varied carrier in terms of land mass than SP. It fights winter's heaviest drifts at a summit in the midst of the nation's greatest single spine, the brutal Sierra Nevada chain, races along below sea level in California where its steel threads hundreds of miles of the driest, hottest terrain out west, as well as being a major player on the agricultural chess board known as the Great Plains. Other railroads beyond the Mississippi River do this, too, but not as extensively as SP, which outreaches everyone else in the railroad business in this respect.

Beyond the California-Arizona line, where Los Angeles Division iron blends into Tucson Division's desert expanse, there is little to describe about SP helper engine assignments. With the exception of an occasional assist for the first few dozen miles east out of the Tucson terminal, there is hardly a formalized definition of a heavy grade, 1.5%. This measurement does not prevail on that substantial rail domain east of El Paso.

Those storied mountain ranges which so dominate an operating department's thinking processes lie west and north of California's verdant Imperial Valley, and throughout the uneven forests of Oregon. So there always seems to be more power assigned to a particular division on the road's west end than in the east.

Slower trains, a mountain-style specialty, soak up the roster lists. SP

Opposite: With Ashland only a few mileposts behind, four helpers are working for all their worth as a trainload of lumber products begins the long journey south on the California-Oregon crossing of the Siskiyou Range.

73

over the years has always seemed to have a slightly higher ratio of motive power out of service than other western carriers, a circumstance undoubtedly tied to its association with both heavy tonnage trains and numerous steep gradients. That sort of train handling is certainly more stressful upon railroad machines than geography is elsewhere in the nation. Alternate spasms of dynamic braking to running in low notches close to minimum continuous speed make for a wearing experience. Where some predominately flatland road might get 20 years out of a road engine before casting it aside, Espee is lucky to record 15.

The difference is in barriers called Sierra Nevada, Cascades, Tehachapi, and others of less fame but similar challenge.

Without much dissent, SP can be considered the motive power kingpin of the west, an expression that fits almost as well on its lines east of El Paso. Commonplace lashups run to six units just to get regular trains from one terminal to the next, and the potent, six-axled examples which are standard on the mountaintops frequently stay on the point to Kansas City, East St. Louis or New Orleans.

One clue to SP's mindset when it comes to helper locomotive assignments is contained in its overall philosophy, which favors long, heavy, fast trains. While other railroads have carved a fairly standardized niche out of the short, frequent train approach to the competitive level, the San Francisco-based carrier has espoused a greater sized but equally speedy approach to its operations. Since heavy tonnage moving swiftly requires large cuts of horsepower, yardmasters pencil in plenty of muscle, so five-and six-unit hookups of red and grey power are necessary to fit that perspective. Then throw in several stiff mountain passes from Oregon on south and east and you have an emerging pattern which places extra muscle midway or at the rear end of so many SP movements.

Since the days of first-generation diesel locomotives, there has not been any really revolutionary change in helper unit fastenings. The technological gamesmanship that has put multiple lashups of diesel units under the throttle hand of a single engineer has not been successfully extended to similar mastery of helper power. Though western roads, especially SP and Burlington Northern, have ordered radio-controlled sets of master-slave units in recent years, they have not been an outstanding success, if empirical evidence is any measure. The 8300 series of SD-40s, which are split between master and remote-controlled examples, were extensively tried out following their 1974 delivery date. In the 1980s, however, it is rare to see them linked in train service as intended, except perhaps on the Modoc Line from Oregon to Nevada desert reaches.

Overall results with RC units have not been spectacular, or by this time one would have expected a much greater ability. Obviously, there are many technical reasons: difficulty in propagating clear signals through twisting canyons, and the typical problems of slack action while mastering momentum from a remote location in an environment where "touch" is so important in controlling brute energy.

Collectively, the remote linking of locomotives seems to remain a perplexing issue, or, why are there still so many engineers riding the extra ones?

The outstanding example of massive power assigned routinely to uphill operations is found in Southern California, astride the physical break between the San Joaquin Valley and Los Angeles' populous basin. It is called Tehachapi, a railroad spectacular of herculean proportions with a history founded upon applied force.

In its past, SP did one thing over the Tehachapis which was quite rare just about anywhere that helpers roamed: two cab-forward mallets were tied together on the head end of standard equipment, heavyweight passenger trains like the *Owl* and *West Coast*. There was a systemwide prohibition of this method on freight trains, as drawbars couldn't stand the combined tractive effort. But for a short period in the aftermath of World War II it was a standard procedure, illustrating a point about motive power use on the Tehachapi Subdivision that continues to prevail throughout the diesel locomotive generation. It is that this district was and is a prolific user of the heaviest tractive effort cuts while simultaneously being a place for experimentation.

From first to second generation, and in between, Southern Pacific has been noted for its changing opinions of what kind or how much power to slip on behind the road engine, or, for that matter, ahead of it. Certainly it was that way on Tehachapi. During pre-Amtrak times the dwindling passenger train schedule was finally down to a *San Joaquin Daylight,* run daily in each direction. Early on it had been assigned orange and red PAs, but it ultimately wound up with mundane freight-style A-B-B combines of the Black Widow look, concluding with 205-ton SDP45s. The latter easily handled what had become a truncated varnish rub, but prior to that a diversified group of diesels had been seen aiding the daily passenger schedule over the famed Tehachapi Loop and its difficult approaches.

It was not uncommon during the PA era to find less colorful Alco products, say a jet black RSD5, going coupler to coupler with No. 51 or 52, as the San Joaquin was ID'd in its number boards. Upon arrival of F-7s as standard road power, helpers of a similar shadow seemed to become commonplace, while reduced cars and higher horsepower SDP-45s did away with the notion entirely. This affair was relatively short-lived when Amtrak came along and decided the long way from Bakersfield to Los Angeles by way of a mountain pass was not a competitive setting.

Centralizing today's railroad has brought growth of limited proportions to a few locations. For the most part, however, as Southern Pacific and every other major railroad have followed this pattern, outlying terminals have been downgraded. Bakersfield Yard in the San Joaquin Valley's

Sometimes a light train is just a bit over the tonnage ratings for a grade and a single unit is all that's needed. Tied on the rear of a caboose so it can be uncoupled on the fly a lone U33C pushes uphill in the Tehachapis.

southernmost city, a place where the mountain begins, has undergone this transformation. The old brick roundhouse which lasted a couple of decades beyond flat-faced ACs is now gone, as are many other system facilities which until even five years ago had proved useful in the scheme of pushing trains aloft to high desert country.

That hasn't stopped the heavy tonnage types speeding down the smooth Valley floor from Fresno and beyond. Braking heavily at the yard limit board, they paused while amid the regimen of changing crews a four- or five-unit clan of SD40-45s will be cut in mid-train or perhaps a solo sort will be hooked to an air hose in back of a caboose or a last car.

In 1985 the mountain is basically all EMD, but till a few years back a considerably greater assortment was at hand. For years a relatively few SD-38s and SD-39s owned by SP held forth between Los Angeles and Bakersfield, or even to Colton when the Palmdale Cut-off became reality. By early 1985 a few of these that had not been traded in were working elsewhere. The 5300-series SD-39s, for example, were sent over to the coast for helper service on Cuesta grade where their well-worn bodies weren't so heavily taxed on that much shorter climb.

Tehachapi's often walled-in sidings throbbed routinely to the discordant beat of GE U30Cs and U33Cs which were almost more stereotyped on some days than even LaGrange products. These models were just as prone to helper assignments as were SD-9s before them.

A 1970s era on Tehachapi would be mostly U-boats. A month later it seemed they had fled elsewhere, while quite a few Nines had been brought in, suggesting a temporary mainline power shortage somewhere on SP's vast spread, momentarily gobbling up all the high horsepower units.

76

Four weeks later six-axled heavies were there again in numbers, and so it has gone from year to year, right to the present.

There seems to be endless innovation.

The latest wrinkle has been the dedicated helper, a set of power kept together between Bakersfield and West Colton for trips on end, unlike a more typical time-honored practice where *ad hoc* cuts of diesels were simply grabbed off each ready track in required combos of brawn, then attached to a train. With helpers kept together in assigned blocks it is felt there is better planning for trains expected to need them during the next 24 hours.

Inroads in recent years have reduced a bit of the need for supporting mountain-bound trains. Some of this stems from the creation of the all-trailer/container-style hotshot which so dominates 1980s railroading. With their relatively light weight strewn along skeleton-framed cars, the contemporary hotshots neither need nor receive massive doses of helper power. Generally a single six-axled example will suffice to boost a train up and

Back in the '60s there was more early generation power in helper service as evidenced by this trio of SD-9s (unrebuilt) plugging away through Walong.

over the Sierras or from the southern San Joaquin Valley up the brown grass slopes of Tehachapi.

But the heavier boxcar-dominated runs are still much as in earlier diesel age times; three or more helper units are needed to overcome drag that a climbing, circuitous barrier can impose upon their course.

Come now to a recent night on Tehachapi Mountain, one tiny bit of a great railroad with lots of round-the-clock moves. At the moment, an inbound Cotton Belt waits patiently outside its terminal in East St. Louis, headlight staring at a duo of Terminal Railroad Association switchers dragging a lengthy interchange movement into an ICG facility. Two thousand miles west, by northwest on Oregon Division, a train is all wrapped up in the woods, a glimmer of moving lights here and there in the often damp Cascade Mountains where mostly owls are awake.

On the Southern California mountain, one of the most dramatic, most intriguing and busiest stretches on anybody's railroad is engaged in routine action. A few rays of light pierce what is otherwise a colorless void.

Wham!

What had been four six-motored jobs plugging away on Tehachapi's upgrade at the east end of Bealville has in an instant of escaping air slowed to a crawl, then halted and turned totally still. So sudden is the contrast that it leaves a half-drowsy spectator in momentary wonderment.

Derailment perhaps?

An instant later a decelerating helper is heard, its dwindling cadence drifting out beyond a chain of deep cuts while train speed is falling off to nothing. More prominent now are the creaks and groans of running gear.

All is silent; the head end is beyond one curve, with helpers buried somewhere behind. Moments later a glimmer of light appears from where the lead engine is hidden; it pauses to check draft gear of one car, then moves in methodical sequence to another and another. This is no derailment. A dragging equipment indicator at Bealville has sensed something, and as the head end curled around a sharp curve to enter tunnel No. 5 it encountered a flashing red light, so the hogger just shut it down, coasting to a quick, effortless stop on the uphill.

Five minutes, 10 minutes slip by. This ought to be pretty good!

Both roads on Tehachapi, SP and Santa Fe, have calculated—at least in theory—that any train dispatched uphill out of Bakersfield, or less often out of Mojave, can get out of any siding it has to. It's only a matter of horsepower-to-weight ratios.

Well and good, but any experienced railroader knows that what should happen and what does are often mismatched. A sub-par unit, slippery rail, unexpected slack action, a dozen other events, and it's going to be difficult getting out of a mountain siding with a few thousand inert tons snaked around numerous curves.

Now almost imperceptibly air brakes are being released, so the moment of truth is at hand. Hidden in meandering fashion on this piece of sharply tumbling mountainside, SP's freight must be heavy, if it's a normal boxcar specimen, for this railroad's ideal runs to length and brute force, climb or not.

This show has got to be exciting because almost immediately a wheel is turned, the lead unit's nose is inside a curved tunnel, followed by a series of sharp, ascending curls that opens upon a hanging cliff.

Just getting in gear again is dramatic.

So it proves to be from one end to the other.

Sand in tiny rivulets spews ahead of steel rims an instant before they inch ahead in a first tentative assault on inertia. First by fractions, then yards, they bite into a darkened Tehachapi. A smell of burnt diesel fuel floats backward on a gentle breeze, as units plunge into a short tunnel where sights and sounds become bottled up. Momentarily, only passing freight cars generate any sort of sound, but it isn't long before a helper is heard, which, based upon Espee standards, will likely prove a hefty one.

Road engine and helper alike are really pushing it now, clawing for every foot of altitude up ahead. Bursting from a cut the helper is seen to be mid-train, not tail end, so there must be a long train here. Two sets of white running board lights . . . three, four, now five, then another . . . six in all. A glance at their faint silhouettes indicates four SD-45s, two 40s, slightly more than 20,000 horsepower total.

Some railroads have never put that much power onto a single train. Southern Pacific has calculated it in a helper locomotive.

The noise is deafening. Nearby ground shudders underfoot with each few yards as the pace quickens, though it will never be speedy on the hill. From a dead start to 15 or 20 mph in a train length, even a long one, is performance enough.

One instinctively knows, despite the dark, that it is an SP train, for Santa Fe thinks differently, settling on shorter, lighter trains, many of which climb unaided up both sides, while others may get one or two units. Perhaps once in a while "Uncle John" might call on a heftier cut of units, but they'll probably be four-axled types on a break from the valley.

As Southern Pacific's independence possibly draws to a conclusion the current champ is a train known in slang as the "oil cans." A solid unit train of 72 large tank cars, it shuttles between Bakersfield and a Shell Oil Co. refinery in the Los Angeles Harbor, on an every other day circle.

A measure of what kind of massive power the "oil cans" expect is seen in the half-dozen six-motored units pulling an empty train going north out of Los Angeles. This is due to a climb through Soledad Canyon and the short but steep part of Tehachapi Pass on the east slope beyond Mojave. Imagine then what it takes to thrust a *loaded* train up and over heavily canted curves and rising roadbed found on the longer western flank. Try a total of 11 or 12 of EMD's heaviest types digging in for all they're capable of, and you have a picture that's rarely duplicated anywhere else, particularly on an almost everyday basis.

Channeled thunder roars up and down the confines of Tehachapi Creek, bursts beyond frequent tunnels or just plain blasts uphill in unison. The decibel production of a dozen big ones in full throat has to be experienced to be comprehended.

It is a mood seldom expressed beyond the mileposts of Southern Pacific.

Whether or not a merged SP-SF would have continued to call upon booster power to this extent is problematical. For many years Santa Fe has reduced its quota of helpers on eastbounds out of Bakersfield, in good part because it has been so thoroughly converted to a dominant piggyback trade as well as abridged train size. Generally, the nature of its traffic sources is a bit different from SP's, which has many full-bodied trainloads of forest products out of Oregon with their heavier consists. On the average, only the heaviest Santa Fe runs are boosted eastbound, a relatively junior ranking in the 1980s. Nor is the short/fast concept geared to extra physique.

Four engines plus short trains will do quite well even on the maximum 2.2% rise from the San Joaquin Valley. If a converted ideology toward abbreviated length ever takes over on SP divisions, perhaps even fewer moves will be hitched to added horsepower. Some indication that this is the future lies in a rumor that a complete double tracking is due between Bakersfield and Mojave, filling in the few miles between mountain sidings now listed as 68 miles of operational single track. Possibly there will be more, shorter trains to occupy it.

Elsewhere on the West Coast there are other helper districts, some shorter, some longer than Tehachapi, but nothing as frequent or as active. The chorus is swelled by light movements downhill into Bakersfield. At times two or three helpers will be held at Summit Switch, a crossover as well as the apex of the hill, coupled together and returned as a single move.

Since July 11, 1967, SP has been sending its trains into a breach in Southern California's San Bernardino Mountains, better known to railroaders as Cajon Pass. Famed for its historical placement on Santa Fe's main stem, Cajon Pass represented a way in which SP could avoid the growing delay and congestion associated with its burgeoning Los Angeles Basin terminal, primarily its long-standing Taylor Yard near downtown Los Angeles. Coupled with the creation of its giant yard at outlying West Colton in the early '70s, this route provided a quicker, smoother link with Northern California and Oregon.

Its finalization also meant a fresh helper district of modest length but sharp proportions.

As with other districts on the West Coast to which helpers are assigned, a varied rationale and motive power look have been featured as part of

80

Cajon. The introductory approach was to affix extra power first at Colton, then West Colton when the new yard came into being, running them to the top of Cajon Pass whereupon they returned light, or to a lower siding to await another train to assist. This meant about a 27-mile-long shove over a fair amount of 2% gradient to Hiland, the uppermost point, which corresponds to Santa Fe's better-known tip at Summit.

In recent years many trains have been assigned through-helpers covering the full 181-mile span of the Mojave Subdivision from Bakersfield to West Colton, so that an engineer gets to test his mettle on two of the most famous railroad passes in America, Cajon and Tehachapi, in a single run.

Yet another helper district astride Southern California's matrix is also launched from West Colton. It goes through nearby San Timeteo Canyon to Beaumont on eastbounds, and from Indio or thereabouts to Beaumont

Returning light from a trip with the oil train, six units slip through the siding at Bealville, soon drawing up to an absolute signal at the lower end power switch where they'll hold for a Santa Fe train coming the other way.

When Kaiser Steel still melted ore at its Fontana Mill, SP provided the iron from a connection with Eagle Mountain Railway on the Salton Sea shoreline. To get the short but heavy train through Beaumont Pass a helper set became an absolute necessity.

on trains heading west. This pass is known as San Gorgonio Pass, or Beaumont Pass, depending upon what source is chronicled.

Indio used to be the division point for this area as well as a terminal for helpers, but several years ago it was bypassed and crews now run through from West Colton to Yuma. The east end helper district is longer, 52 miles Indio-Beaumont versus 27 miles West Colton, while in both instances units are frequently added at sidings further up the line, shortening the total push. For instance, the heavy demands for westbounds begin at Garnet, with sidings at Salvia, Rimlon, Thousand Palms and Myoma located between there and Indio. Any of them can be used by a dispatcher to meet a train and its helper although the one at Thousand Palms shows off a 21,029-foot length, and is the most convenient, since two trains can fit in at once.

To a certain extent Beaumont Pass is one of those stretches of mountain which because of its key position has been almost double tracked over the years. In fact, the shorter, west side drop into West Colton, is. If a few power switches were lashed together on the desert floor between Indio and Beaumont, you would have that kind of railroad now.

The West Colton scene typically finds a helper added outside the yard at Loma Linda, six miles east of the yard and past the new Santa Fe con-

82

nection which is being forged at the site of old Colton Tower. If SP-SF had become a reality the two roads would have blended their traffic into and out of Southern California, with the new switches being spiked down prominent in this changed order. Meanwhile, hundreds of cars daily clatter across the old diamond, many stopping just east of the old yard where a set of weatherbeaten grey units with ambitious intentions is thrown into the consist, if only briefly.

Choke point on the Coast!

That might be a dispatcher's impressionable retort when someone mentioned San Luis Obispo in discussing operations between Los Angeles and San Francisco. On the northwest flank of town lies abridged but difficult Cuesta Grade, 17 miles' worth of typical California coastal range that Southern Pacific couldn't avoid.

In recent years operations on the Coast Route between California's two largest cities have been dwindling, despite an occasional seasonal flurry or so. One potential reason is Cuesta, which stands out like a sore thumb on a route that is basically free of any significant gradient and is generally free-flowing though saddled with aging automatic block signals. While Tehachapi has been routinely upgraded over the years the Coast Route is, investment-wise, much the same as when steam departed. As matters stand in the 1980s, the glare of potential merger and the spirit of competition put roadbed between San Francisco and Los Angeles definitely in the category of "also ran," barring the development of Sprint-type traffic between the two big cities.

Cuesta, while abbreviated as a 17-mile pusher district, creates a blocking condition far beyond its scope to smooth train operations. Nor is it a one-way district either since it crests on 2.1% and 2.2% slopes from both directions. Even if practical dispatchers try to coordinate both south and northbound trains in such a way that a helper set hammering uphill out of San Luis Obispo will be dropped at Santa Margarita, three miles below the summit, to meet a train coming south out of Watsonville Jct. without undue waiting, he may not be successful.

It seems funny to tack on four, five, even six, helpers to boost a freight but three miles, even over a curt little bit of 2.2% that extends just over a single, short summit.

That, however, is railroading on Cuesta.

Rather than keep several units tied up in San Luis Obispo for the Coast's sometimes infrequent trains, Espee will perhaps run them on a local between there and San Luis Obispo bringing them back in time to provide aid over the Cuesta. If matters aren't coordinated just right someone has to sit for a time, one reason the Coast Route isn't all that popular these days.

No particular day is quite the same as another and just when that kind of statement is made a daily train sheet will alter, but in broad terms the

A weekend scene finds SDP-45 working in helper service through Yuba Pass in the Sierra, a much higher altitude than it normally worked in commute service south of San Francisco.

Coast is less active than San Joaquin Valley subdivisions. Four through freights plus two Amtraks and locals wouldn't be far off a typical performance along with specialized moves such as solid sugar beet trains during summer months and a solid coke train moving from Callender down into Los Angeles and back up to Searles.

Roseville, SP's Northern California hub, is also one leg of a major helper district, the railroad's most celebrated. California's great vertical spine, the looming Sierra Nevada chain, provides a reason, and during steam days Roseville undoubtedly had the busiest roundhouse anywhere on the system. During those times the sheer length of the helper district plus a busier timetable soaked up dozens of locomotives. Then, too, the amount of water a tender could hold limited how far an engine could run. Probably 30 miles and a water tank were a common denominator for each of the three big flat-faced mallets that were a routine consist. Currently, the Overland Route, as the line between the Bay Area and Ogden is called, is

84

seeing much less traffic than before, particularly since Union Pacific acquired its own way into California by way of the Western Pacific.

There have been times recently when an eight-hour stint on this "hill" might produce a single freight past any particular point. Next day a similar time lapse might record six or seven.

Like so many other trunk-type subdivisions, Roseville Sub across the Sierra is subject to bunching. Other variables exist, as they do elsewhere, making train scheduling an uneven process at best. Much traffic tends to move eastward on the Sierra hump at night, reflecting release times for trailer/container-type traffic from the Bay region. Departing quickly at day's end, trains are well out on the Nevada desert by early morning.

Stem to stern, Roseville's mountainous subdivision is a double-tracked railroad across its 156-mile-long haul, making this transmountain obstacle unsurpassed on Southern Pacific. Again, as with other heavy-duty sections of SP, helper usage has dwindled in the face of technological change in rolling stock and the advent of intermodal traffic in solid concentrations. In quite a few instances the upshot is a single unit behind a caboose draw-bar instead of three units buried deeper or at the last car if no crummy is attached. On heavy trains, those of more traditional form, the old standard still prevails, though they dwindle in number with each passing year.

Due to its size and total double tracking, the Sierra's majestic district is most unusual insofar as SP is concerned and probably on the overall American scene as well. With certain exceptions at the top of the hill there are no meets to take place, with a pusher of whatever size being attached at Roseville or Sparks, Nevada, depending upon direction. It works away uninterrupted until turned loose when its mission is complete. There are relatively few unexpected delays on the Sierras other than those that accompany winter snowstorms, a foreseeable event. With them a 37-mile segment of roadbed containing snow sheds, tunnels and crossovers over the mountaintop from Truckee to Emigrant Gap is tagged as an interlocking zone permitting great flexibility, particularly during those winter months when flangers or rotary plows are called out to keep things stirring.

At times like these there's no telling how often or for how long a train might be stopped or be moved in intermittent jumps.

Otherwise you can create a formula of tonnage, motive power plus distance traveled to calculate a climb over the Sierras and predict almost within a few minutes when a several thousand ton freight will arrive at the opposite terminal. Well, almost, if there are no break-in-twos, dragging brakes, broken air hoses and the like to mar ambitions.

Pattern-wise the lengthy helper zone displays a wide variety of hook-ups over the years, as well as at present. As previously mentioned, a popular method in the 1980s is a single rear-end unit back of the last car, a connection which allows the locomotive to be detached on the fly at Norden if such proves desirable. Still on any given day you'll undoubtedly see more than one train with three, four or even more units assisting uphill. Tonnage and a freight's priority will be the determinant.

Southern Pacific cards a unit train of cement hoppers and spasmodic coal trains westbound across the mountain and into Bay Area destinations. There's no way a single diesel set will suffice in these circumstances and a coal run was observed in early 1986 with a six-unit mid-train booster blasting away through Truckee's resort town. The cement train appears deceptively tiny with its collection of short wheelbase hoppers, a look that won't fool a front- or rear-end hogger. They know how heavy it is.

It's difficult to say how long a helper will stay hitched to its train. The west side ascent is long, 86 miles northeastwards from Roseville to the highest point at Norden, although extra power may originally be latched on at Rocklin four miles east of Roseville Yard. A fair amount of the west slope rises above a 2% angle, representing a bare minimum of aid. Frequently helpers are cut out at Norden to return west. Often they stay on all the way downhill through Reno and Sparks.

How many westbounds are due through Sparks? What motive power is available? How heavy are trains? These are facts which determine where engines are split off.

On a side note, SP's jaunt past casino row in Reno and through the multi-story parking building of one casino has to be one of the more unusual railroad settings anywhere.

The westbound pusher district, from Sparks' division point to Norden, is much shorter—54 miles—while running to a maximum 1.8%, with much of it somewhat less.

Balance of power needs often place a larger than expected helper set on westbounds, which includes keeping them aboard as mid-train power all the way downhill into Roseville's massive yard. It depends upon so many variables that no singular pattern emerges, which is what makes the Sierra Nevada haul such an intriguing subdivision.

Can one picture a greater, more abrupt contrast than emerging from the precipitous sound and fury of an imposing mountain barrier, to gaze upon a Nevada's vast desert that expands in limitless fashion to where the earth curves? Or the 180-degree reciprocal?

□

To escape the northern boundary of California's Great Central Valley, SP depends upon another helper district, one not so abruptly present as is Tehachapi at its southern limit. First come a few dozen miles of meandering in company with the Sacramento River in its upper reaches, a narrow V-shaped crevice below spectacular Mt. Shasta. At Dunsmuir well upriver from its beginnings near Redding there is a division point as Sacramento Division iron becomes that of Oregon Division, the "Boxcar Railroad" chronicled elsewhere. Along with a pro-forma crew change many trains heading for Klamath Falls—an eastward jaunt by timetable direction—

receive a helper, usually one, perhaps two units. The heavy trains carrying lumber products move south into California, so returns typically consist of empties plus piggyback trains out of both Los Angeles and San Francisco.

Dunsmuir can bustle. The intermodal traffic daily in both directions, plus a pair of Amtrak schedules between Seattle and Southern California, represent priority traffic that is steady. Oregon's chief commodity, wood, at times displays a checkered existence. Sawmills can be humming, producing reams of box and flatcars to spawn trains, or business can be flat with hours ticking off a standard clock with nary a train crew being called.

When train action is really hot, 20 to 25 trains in a 24-hour cycle wouldn't be that unusual. Keep in mind this is single track, CTC and mountain grade all compressed into a natural spectacle, summer or winter.

The heavy ones will need a boost, a helper trailing out back as they edge cautiously into a sharp curve, abruptly disappearing into an extremely circuitous routing to gain altitude before emerging upon a more expansive, yet less woodsy plain that carries through the town of Mt. Shasta, 14 forested miles past Dunsmuir. Not far beyond Dunsmuir track turns back upon itself to keep grade down, a feature known as Cantara Loop, but in truth really a hairpin turn. At times, instead of plugging into a consist right out of Dunsmuir's charming canyon dwelling locale the helper will pick up its train at Black Butte, a marvelous little junction near the town of Weed.

In recent years Southern Pacific has maintained room at Black Butte to rest a few engines, either for helper service to Grass Lake or for the daily Siskiyou Subdivision freight that connects with southern Oregon at Ashland. Typically on Klamath Falls trains a helper will stay on to Grass Lake, 23 miles past the junction along a climbing, coiling circuit that works its way through the lower slopes of Mt. Shasta. Once in a while an engine may drift past Grass Lake to assist a train climbing the opposite way. Usually they just return light to Black Butte or Dunsmuir.

As helper country, the Siskiyou Line provides one more among many facets of SP's diverse habits. Routinely, there is a single, often quite long weekday train daily each way between Dunsmuir–Black Butte and Ashland, 85 miles away. A three- to four-unit mid-train helper operates through along with a road engine of similar size. The bulk of energy is expended getting into and out of Ashland in both directions and on a nasty little grade just before Black Butte that slows down matters considerably for southbound freights.

One curiosity of the Ashland–Black Butte–Dunsmuir freight is that in both directions a fair amount of switching may be performed at Black Butte on a curving, descending group of tracks. SP moved some switching out of Dunsmuir itself and up the mountain to Black Butte several years ago.

As a measure of the difference between mountain subs and flatland consider that for other than very hot trains the standard maximum-per-ton horsepower ratio down in Texas on the Valentine Subdivision is 2.0, while on Dunsmuir–Grass Lake or Black Butte–Ashland it is 6.0.

There is a distinction.

North of Ashland, particularly beyond Grants Pass on the way to Eugene's retarders, Siskiyou Subdivision roadbed is a succession of forested crests with any sort of tangency a cause for curiosity. A healthy set of six-axled units on the point will normally prove sufficient, but it is not unknown for loaded freights to be assigned a helper. For slow, often tortuous mainline railroading that frequently alternates between the lowest throttle notches and wailing dynamic braking, there is little that is comparable.

Repeatedly, Southern Pacific serves up a different look.

At its north end Oregon Division is laced with branch lines, feed stock for Eugene's clattering hump lead. In 3-D they would stand out as lines dipping into tree-carpeted flanks on either side of the broad Willamette Valley. As such they are occasional if not regular candidates for inclusion in the roster of helper districts. Unfortunately in this entire region the annual carloadings generated by lumber mills have been dwindling, so the often long, extremely heavy trains of yesteryear are a declining circumstance. However, it still takes a well-muscled set of SDs to hack away at a branch line's often rugged physique.

Busiest district for helpers on Oregon Division is a mainline setting, lying between Eugene's large terminal and Cascade Summit, 113 miles of difficult single track. Not all snowstorms visit Norden, either, for Odell Lake and environs at the top of SP's long, upward trek share the same winter wonderland. In actuality few helpers will be tied in at Eugene, even as road crews pick up their motive power there. Habitually the helper will run ahead of a through move, waiting at one of a few sidings west of Oakridge to start work, for that's where the real chore begins, reducing a twin locomotive train to only the heftiest 50 miles.

Having assisted one train up the mountain, a helper crew may be called upon to repeat the performance from Oakridge, if there's time left. Helping is an extended, slow performance in the Cascades with many crews reaching their hours of service limit before getting back to Eugene. In that case SP will dispatch a taxi to meet them, probably at the top where road access is available, because there are many sidings that aren't accessible. In winter forget it entirely.

Typical of mountain railroading, this Cascade subdivision is mostly routine train handling that never rules out the unexpected. It's expected!

At one juncture till SP recently abandoned a major portion of its Northwestern Pacific Railroad route north of Willits, California. A short helper district whose backbone was SD-9s stretched over a wall in the Coastal Mountains. It ran from Willits south 17 miles to Redwood Valley. That portion of abandoned rail to the north was taken over by a shipper-

owned short line, feeding carloads to SP at Willits. Since traffic is down considerably on this line the use of helpers is too.

Finally, there is Ogden, Utah. On westbound coal drags there is usually at least a single unit to Valley Pass, ditto for weighty grain trains as they cross the Salt Lake fill and disappear into the Nevada desert, often through to Carlin. After crossing Lucin Cut-off fill, SP encounters about a hundred miles of heavy-duty hill country, including two extended grades.

In the spring of 1986 a severe storm partially wrecked the west end of Lucin Cut-off's Great Salt Lake fill, shutting down the line for two months while interrupting the continuous grading work that had been going on for some length. With the lake gradually rising to historic elevations the railroad had been running two and three work trains each day, attempting to keep the fill above climbing waters.

During the shutdown SP utilized Union Pacific roadbed at the lake's south end, itself subject to the same forces and solution.

Once track was reopened, Espee went back to its original chore, operating a clutch of daily rockfill locals for the foreseeable future. That is as long as the lake keeps rising.

An occasional helper assignment westbound, somethings across the entire 248-mile-long Salt Lake Subdivision to Carlin.

Ultimately there is the unforeseen, a Southern Pacific specialty.

Don't be surprised to come across a locomotive in helper service just about anywhere that red and grey units shake the ballast. Given this railroad's great familiarity with the breed, it won't hesitate to dispatch them in places and during moments when they're least predicted.

Four tunnel motors occupy center stage on this Siskiyou Line train which has just passed over the hardest phase of its Ashland–Black Butte run, a few miles of 3.3% on both sides of the crest.

89

A hazy morning lying over Cajon Pass hides a mountainous backdrop, while a heavy, slow sugar beet extra works its way over the Palmdale Cut-off with a combo of Geeps and U30Cs providing an assist.

A modest-sized two-unit helper consisting of an SD-45 from EMD and an RSD-15 from Alco pair up for a mid-train chore.

Opposite: The heavy lumber packed trains that come south from Oregon always need a big helper to get over the Tehachapis and on this particular day in the mid-1970s it was an all-GE set of four units that was sandwiched into the middle.

THE VALLEY

Railroading, California style

TWO NATURAL ROUTES between Los Angeles and San Francisco beckoned railroads in their formative years. Highway and airlines would logically mimic them in their own time.

In expressive, uncomplicated terms those routes are known as the Coast and the Valley and Southern Pacific occupies both. The one that suggests water has no particular geographic feature by which it is identified, while the other is very much an outstanding natural feature; the Great Central Valley of California, an agricultural belt with decades of influence upon the state's railroads, especially SP and Santa Fe.

In terms of familiar names, Bakersfield on the south, Dunsmuir a bit into the mountains up north, and Roseville, laid at the doorstep of the precipitous Sierra Nevada, plus San Francisco Bay, define its limits. All railroad towns to a degree, but not everything. Fresno, Stockton, Modesto, Redding all compute strongly in the contemporary language of CRTs at One Market Street. Each has its quota of locals, drags and hotshots, the substance of what a large railroad is all about. All are part of the Valley.

Important in their own right, these places act as bridge country to other parts of the nation and the world. The brightest star currently shining over western railroads is that "land bridge" concept wherein shiploads of containers become trains, trundled between ocean ports and their east-gulf coast counterparts. On round-trip waybills to meet ships at either end, Valley roadbed is part of the conduit, south by way of Bakersfield and Tehachapi, or a quick cross-town hike to the Sierra's massive wall.

Geologically, the elongated valley averaging 60 to 70 miles in width north to south is a singular physical feature. Popularly there is a loose split. South of Stockton SP describes its right-of-way as railroading through the *San Joaquin Valley,* above that the *Sacramento Valley* exists to Redding where it butts against the Sacramento River, which spills from a narrow crevasse into Shasta Dam, and then the plain below. To either

Opposite: An early SD-45 rebuild leads a trio of tunnel motors through Kern Jct. on a cloudy day in the southern San Joaquin Valley. The old wooden tower which lay astride the SP–ATSF junction has recently been torn down.

93

elongated flank, as foothills mature into mountains, the main line throws out branch lines to tap them. The major outlet to the west extends through delta country, a watery maze of low-lying land that spreads from Stockton-Sacramento to bayside piers.

Certain patterns emerge from SP's central California playbook. Traffic for Sacramento Division on the Overland Route comes north from mid-valley sources. Off the Coast, mostly the north end; from Northwestern Pacific Railroad, the Bay Area, and out of Oregon, especially the Siskiyou Line as some Cascade Line cars move via Alturas Line steel. Then there's Bay Area-Northwest activity, some moving through the West Valley Line's non-CTC territory, some traveling through Roseville and up the East Valley Line to Marysville. Threading through this is Southern California's connection to the Northwest, the bulk of trains being sent through Roseville in both directions. Alternatives do abound as a map check will illustrate. Traffic between Fresno and Tracy-Martinez can always take the West Side Line, a block-signaled secondary way which can offer routing for medium-speed trains with its 40-mph subdivision maximum.

For all the major Valley and Bay Area trunk lines of Southern Pacific there is no need to mention "gradient." A branch or two that climbs into the western foothills of the Sierra Nevada, maybe, but that's all. The key to railroading in the Valley is siding lengths, rail weight and proper spacing of trains *plus* keeping locals in their proper place.

Three Southern Pacific divisions combine to create an abundance of trains in the Valley's core. From the Fresno arena down the valley to Bakersfield and over the Tehachapi barrier, San Joaquin Division authority is paramount. Generally north of Fresno to Sacramento (midstate) and to Dunsmuir (the north end), Sacramento Division has the reins, while the Western Division, which blankets San Francisco Bay with its look, shoots a pair of tentacles upriver towards Tracy and Sacramento. Clearly dominating the great natural feature are the first two, spreading out across several hundred miles of mostly single track. Overall it is Southern Pacific, the departments being mere technicalities for those establishing train symbols and schedules.

With SP, a railroad that basically originates more eastbound traffic out of the West Coast and the Southeast than it does the reverse, San Joaquin-Sacramento Valley terminals get their quota of empties moving in from other locations, especially from beyond the Colorado River. A not unusual northbound run is a complete train of "light" cars; boxes, flats, plaster flats, *et al.,* spilling out of Bakersfield and destined for Eugene, a byproduct of Oregon's lumber industry with its one-way tradition. Secondly—and this is a matter that affects every SP terminal from East St. Louis to Portland's Brooklyn Yard—there is always the "Two-Sunday Wave." This has an impact upon central California, where traffic is heavy on Sundays, while toward midweek westbound tonnage drops, as fewer

Flat and fast, the San Joaquin Valley's agricultural heritage stands over the fleeting image of a high-speed freight heading westbound to Fresno.

cars come across the Mississippi River. The oftimes spotty density of freights on San Joaquin-Sacramento Division steel is thus explained.

To which is added a complex seasonal factor, given the multiple agricultural product line of California.

One might expect to come across large numbers of pure four-axle sets working Valley lines, as on mileposts east of El Paso. Other than locals, an occasional GP-40 or B30-7 working away between larger engines, it won't be. The six-axled locomotives that challenge Tehachapi, the Sierra and Oregon country stay put from stem to stern. Matter of fact, you probably won't see much of General Electric anywhere north, the railroad preferring to assign them for maintenance purposes to the shops east of Los Angeles. That has been true for years, even in the heyday of the big sixes from Erie. North of San Francisco or Roseville was and is EMD land, right from the first generation.

There might be one less unit on flatland trains, yet Fresno, Stockton, Tracy, Roseville and other midstate terminals display predominant clusters of what until recently has been SP's favorite locomotive, six-axled brawn.

A dozen years ago, the Valley, the Coast and San Francisco Bay all sported centers of switching and mainline action that have since been shifted, downgraded and modified in the changing panorama of big-time railroads. Among these, Bakersfield, Stockton, Tracy, Bayshore in San Francisco and Watsonville Jct. on the Coast still remain, though their image has dimmed a mite.

Seasonally, Valley trackage used to hum to long strings of solid reefers, both SP and Santa Fe handling thousands of iced cars every season. These days much of what is still produced on nearby fields goes by road or to an intermodal terminal where rubber-tired trailers are lifted aboard a spindly cluster of I-beams mounted on steel wheels. The Santa Fe

95

reefers are all gone now, that road having scrapped the last ones in 1985. SP still uses them but compared to other years the volume is way down. In many instances they serve as mere boxcars, diesel-powered cooling motors silent. On occasion—SP has been out marketing lately—a cut of several operating reefers presents itself to a yardmaster. Almost solid reefer blocks have been known to cross the Sierra during 1986, but considerably more perishables move in aluminum trailers these days, hopefully by train.

Transcontinental traffic waybilled Southern Pacific will for the most part move out south, exiting over the mountains to a hookup with the Sunset or Golden State Routes. Logic says so as SP earns its greatest revenue cut this way. So whether from the Northwest, Bay Area or Central California you would see most loads handled through Bakersfield, making that direction generally busier than by way of Reno and Ogden.

Local runs, on a par with Oregon timber branches or Houston's petroleum sidings, are very much a part of Valley railroading. Systemwide, a typical weekday will see SP operating over 250 such trains, many in the middle of the night. Some will pull no more than 40 to 50 miles while on duty, but they may run to that many car lengths before a crew marks off. For every "through" one, how many locals, how many switch engines were involved?

The Valley may be a shade more strung out, a bit more seasonal in local trains, but they mark the first step.

Unlike the sterile acronyms imposed upon interdivisional runs, locals on SP still reflect a more colorful set of titles. In summer months San Joaquin Valley phone lines ring with a dispatcher querying about such creatures as the Tracy Turn, the Day-Lodi, Nite-Westside, Modesto Switcher and Westside Hauler. Descriptive labels tell a lot about what's happening; crews, engines out spotting or collecting cars at packing plants, stubs and sidings. At trick's end they head back to Fresno, Roseville, Modesto, Stockton and the like. Out in full force from early spring to late fall these so-called locals often weigh as much as a full-sized freight before their power cuts off at an arrival track.

Hardly has a blast of escaping air set brakes when a faded grey SW-1500 attaches itself, primed to flat switch at Fresno or Stockton, to hump at Roseville. Five cars in this block, four in another, one for that track, a half-dozen for one next door. Computer-generated printers have long since been aware of the new arrivals, the soft blue type on switch lists instructing a switch crew how to divide, how to consolidate the latest of arrivals.

Transitioned from puzzle pieces into a full-blown train, several batches from scattered origins will go out as an extra. From the central valley these include Roseville-North Platte Perishables (RVNPP), Roseville-Ogden Perishables (RVOGP) for the Sierra routing to Union Pacific or Rio Grande. Other cars head out south, consigned to a

Bakersfield-East St. Louis Perishable symbol by way of southwest desert roadbed. And there's always localized tonnage, at least in the beginning, carded Bakersfield-Roseville Perishable (BKRVP) or Fresno-Roseville Perishable (FRRVP).

Northbound Valley traffic will be consolidated with trains originating out of coastal points such as a WJRVP (Watsonville Jct.-Roseville Perishable).

Mixing with this often heavy regional scene are the TOFC/COFC runs, surmounting the 1,000-mile gap, Portland to Los Angeles, or in more mixed fashion, heading across the upthrust granite block of the Sierra. The Bay Area ports, acting as a doorway to the Pacific Rim create their own impact and trains.

Southernmost of San Joaquin Valley cities, Bakersfield's railroad importance rests upon the Tehachapi Mountains which stand as a blunt wall, closing off the lower end of the valley from Southern California. From steam days until the present its location has been tailor-made for turning helper power, and for being a division point away from Fresno, Los Angeles and, these days, West Colton.

In the 1980s, Bakersfield's terminal has become a victim of SP's drive to contract, to centralize the number of yards. The old roundhouse came down, yard switchers were pulled off, and Bakersfield declined in local

An empty "Oil Cans" train drifts through Bakersfield Yard. Momentarily the terminal is empty of helper power, and only a couple of Geeps off a local can be seen.

terms. Not so its mainline appearance. Trains still come dragging into town in large numbers, from Oregon and Roseville with a stopover in Bakersfield; from West Colton and Los Angeles, and points east. Crews perform their rites of change, and there's usually two or more sets of helpers on hand to conquer the Loop. Much of the former engine terminal is gone, reduced to plain old racks that provide fuel and sand to units stopping over or turned back upon the mountain. Like many other SP facilities there is a lot less in Bakersfield than there was a dozen years ago, leastwise as a terminal.

In no way does this diminish its role as the southernmost hinge in SP's valley blueprint. Seasonal perishable traffic from the lower end of the valley either goes north as a BKRVP (Bakersfield-Roseville Perishable) block or over Tehachapi as a BKESP (Bakersfield-East St. Louis Perishable) block. The block simply means a group of cars going to the same

Backed off in dynamic braking and still smoking from hot wheels, a westbound Santa Fe train trundles by the lead unit of an upbound SP local at a location known as the "Bealville X-Over."

destination. If the block is long enough it becomes a train, otherwise it is attached by chance or by design to freights passing through. For example, a BKESP block of a dozen cars might go to West Colton on a southbound train that originated at Eugene. Humped at West Colton it becomes part of another movement dashing east.

Bakersfield is one end of a local cross-mountain movement labeled informally "The Oilcans," a solid unit train of bulk petroleum that circulates on a tight schedule between the southern San Joaquin Valley city and a Shell Oil refinery in the Los Angeles harbor district. A real heavyweight of a run, it calls for five head-end units and six engines as a mid-train helper. Seeing that kind of motive power, all C-Cs, play it out on the mountain is an unforgettable event.

In terms of height, Tehachapi's 4,000-foot mark pales with the 7,000-foot trail forged by SP over Donner Pass. Otherwise, there is no contest, because for sheer train action, for the dramatic impact of massive power hoisting long trains through twisting, tunneling, climbing rail, nothing can beat the Valley's southern exit.

At Kern Jct., a tower within shouting distance of SP's Bakersfield engine tracks, Santa Fe comes aboard to join in the assault. In tandem, the

Tehachapi is railroad contortion at its best. At the lower end of Bealville's lengthy siding a westbound Santa Fe train passes up an SP one headed in the same direction.

two carriers run out the last few miles of valley operations, a notable difference existing in their approach to the hazy, brown mountains ahead. Suffice it to say that Santa Fe is the short kid on the block shunning extra power on most of its trains. Southern Pacific is the long one. Other than occasional seasonal help, or the extra heavy ones, Santa Fe daily helper assignments are few. Not so SP, with any size from one to five C-Cs added at Bakersfield for the difficult push. Multi-unit helpers are ordinarily mid-train; singles are behind the last car, a caboose if there is one.

Easing out of Bakersfield Yard or coming through Kern Jct. (in the case of Santa Fe) there seems to be little demand upon the prime movers, at least from an outside angle. As the yard limit board recedes, the double-tracked main is bisecting fields. Appearances are deceptive, for as the mountains loom larger, diesels take on a heavier, laboring tone already into some 1% rise. Two tracks fuse to one at Bena Siding where the line curls over the brow of a hill, dips a bit, then settles on a steady upward thrust for 35 miles.

The Mojave Subdivision, which includes the Tehachapi conquest, is like many western lines; inactivity to a half-dozen sidings plugged in succession. Put the same number of trains on either side, tearing through farms north of Bakersfield, swimming through heat haze on high desert east of Mojave, and it seems totally different. A train that can clip off 30 miles in 30 minutes elsewhere will be grinding away at the hill maybe three hours for a similar accomplishment on the ascent—if, and that is unlikely, no siding switches are thrown in its face. Ten-minute spacing on the flats is a like number of miles. Ten on the hill is the next siding back, maybe a couple of miles. Average gap between power switches for 11 sidings, bottom to top in Loop country, is two to three miles.

The great reverse curve at Caliente introduces upbound freights to their stiffest task. From that point on it is a full bore effort over ruling grades that reach 2.3% while twisting, writhing and bending in every conceivable way. Tiptoeing along a cliff, plunging into tunnels, tossing out great chunks of black smoke, at the very least a quartet of units paws for the top in this round-the-clock heartbeat of two vast railroads meeting their extreme challenge.

Tehachapi abounds in acoustical trickery. One moment a train may sound imminently close, only to arrive up to half an hour later. So swiftly does Tehachapi Creek descend from the summit that it is impossible for rails to follow, but as they wind around the hills above echoes float off a natural sounding board. The bellowing exertions of SD-45s screeching through the curve at Caliente can reach the Loop, providing a half hour's look into the future. As a Santa Fe piggybacker rounds Cliff siding the piercing whine of dynamics floats down to an Espee climber holed up at Caliente, the dispatcher preferring to meet there rather than at Bealville.

High density, a great natural challenge, and the mightiest of motive power assignments make Tehachapi an unparalleled study in western railroading technique.

At a rather unimaginative place called Summit, power that is returning to Bakersfield will be cut out. Otherwise, the through helpers stay aboard and a train just zips down the opposite side on double track to Mojave where Santa Fe takes off on its own single-track course, skimming the high desert to Barstow. Southern Pacific follows a similar pattern, desert running to Palmdale where lines diverge; the most used one now skirts the backside of the San Gabriel Mountains to Cajon Pass and descends to West Colton's marshaling yard. The other connects through Soledad Canyon into the San Fernando Valley and Taylor Yard, now reduced to a minor position in Southern California.

A very active extension, the Lone Pine branch runs north out of Mojave to Searles where SP hooks up to the Trona Railway. Full-blown trains of potash and other chemicals—loads out, empties in—move over this line with much of the blocking done in Mojave.

Other than in physical terms, it is difficult to wall off the Great Central Valley of California from anywhere else that Southern Pacific serves. Like other places, it has its own regional peculiarities, ranging from the acronyms of train I.D. to the provincialism of a local switching assignment. The 2nd Arvin or the Buttonwillow are names only a valley-based railroader would know.

When a 90-plus car train slips into Searles, Calif.—where the Trona Ry. meets up with SP—things can get a bit tight. The original builders of this facility never envisioned the diesel age, lengthy cuts of motive power and even longer trains.

Intermittent shortages of modern six-motored units are not uncommon on SP, so a four-unit set of SD-9s was rounded up to handle a Stockton–Bakersfield train, realistically not much of a challenge on the featureless floor of the San Joaquin Valley.

Assigned to Southern California service in their early years, three U30Cs have an SD-35 spliced in as they struggle upwards past a Santa Fe train near Cliff Siding in the Tehachapis.

Opposite: Locked into a steady push on the "Shell" unit train, a six-unit helper gets some attention from a crew member as it snakes through a series of curves near Bealville.

MATRIX

Southern California is SP Country

O N A WARM, HAZY DAY in Southern California when a temperature inversion is present—local code word for smog—there are perhaps a few longtime residents who wistfully recall a transportation era when Pacific Electric's modest fleet of steeplecab freight engines did a lot of terminal legwork. Their goal, to arrange cuts of cars, eventually led to inclusion in Southern Pacific mainline trains.

In their time, the steeplecabs operated over a spiderweb network of both passenger and freight-only lines that radiated to all the important places, till a few years past World War II when PE eventually ran down to corporate oblivion.

As interurbans dwindled to naught the freight gathering significance of PE achieved a longer running importance in its own right. Though it has been more than 20 years since SP incorporated the electric lines into its own system, much of what was a juice line is today part of a far-reaching terminal operation that extends from just below the mountain passes of Cajon and Beaumont all the way to the beaches of the Pacific Ocean. It encompasses new yards, old yards, exclusive trailer train terminals, cutoffs, plus dozens of lashups of diesels on ready tracks, the whole being netted together by electronics which so dominate and govern contemporary scenes.

In Southern California, SP is in fact a railroad within a railroad, a matrix which most lines have never experienced because they never held title to a complex of steel-trailed branches around which grew a great metropolis. Neither Santa Fe nor Union Pacific can claim anything close to it in the area, nor is there a closely parallel situation elsewhere in the nation. Certainly there are terminal roads, Chicago Belt, Elgin, Joliet & Eastern and St. Louis Terminal Railroad, to name a few which in the past have provided access to industrial districts along with their interchange

Opposite: Rolling up Alameda Street near downtown Los Angeles, a quartet of 5300s brings some local traffic out of the harbor area, bound for the remnants of Taylor Yard.

105

action. But there was only one Pacific Electric and when Southern Pacific fused a network of what had become freight-only lines into its own Los Angeles Division in 1965, the territory it created became a very busy complex of train action unparalleled anywhere else on the system.

And in this projected year of doubt about Southern Pacific's independence, change continues to make its presence felt. There is the normal kind of change that has been going on for decades in this ever-growing region, and the more recent kind, from consolidation plans based upon the merger, now derailed. Rumors fly that this or that facility will cease to be, or at very least find itself downgraded. This line will go, this one will get busier.

Come back in five years and see. By then, suggestions, decisions will have become fact.

During mid-1985 the "Company"—as employees traditionally term their source of income—made some moves in and around the Los Angeles Basin that initially seemed surprising. Actually, they were set in motion some years before, upon completion of the Palmdale Cut-off and the subsequent creation of outlying West Colton Yard. The railroad closed down Taylor Yard's long-standing hump yard, its principal local facility until West Colton was created in a flat field.

Although Taylor was converted to a hump yard in 1949 and had classified thousands of trains, its dwindling role in recent years was confirmed by its closure. Realistically, its demise as the linchpin was confirmed when the railroad took the high road through Cajon Pass, putting much north-south traffic outside the terminal's trackage. In 1973, upon completion of West Colton Yard as the nation's most advanced facility, the ultimate decline of Taylor was a foregone conclusion. Its hump had become surplus as West Colton took over mastery of train assembly, and with most Northern California tonnage running around it by way of Cajon Pass there wasn't all that much to keep its retarders working hard, just Coast Line traffic and a reduced volume of business up Soledad Canyon to Bakersfield and the Great Central Valley.

Taylor Yard, sited a few miles north of downtown Los Angeles, had stood for years as the indispensable Los Angeles Basin focus from which everything in and out of town had to pass. The first crack in that pattern appeared when City of Industry was blessed with a new yard. An industrial-type complex east of El Monte, the Industry facility was strategically located with reference to Orange County and the Los Angeles Harbor district. A link was forged by way of Union Pacific track to Los Nietos, an ex-Pacific Electric yard.

It meant that a lot of traffic which formerly came out of the harbor over the onetime PE four-track trunk into Taylor Yard for classifying could now avoid that often crowded spot while meeting the main line at City of Industry. Gradually, inbound and outbound trains grabbed fill or

dropped off larger and larger cuts of cars at that point which is located 18 miles due east of downtown Los Angeles. When Eagle Mountain Mine iron ore was being exported to Japan, solid strings of squat, heavily loaded hoppers clattered through Los Nietos to Long Beach; but as the trailer/container train grew in importance, full trainloads of skeleton-like flats put in an appearance, till today a substantial volume of area-wide movements bypasses the original Southern California pattern of dispatching, i.e., out of Taylor Yard.

Unlike West Colton, which was built from the ground up as a sophisticated terminal to start off 100% contemporary from Day One, Taylor Yard is more representative of the close-to-downtown facility that many railroads across the nation still hang onto. After World War II it was converted to a hump yard, then as steam gave way to diesels, there was a large diesel running and rebuild shop, although some of the old engine servicing buildings were retained because they were useful. Then, this improvement

With a pair of cabooses in tow, a switcher leaves Taylor Yard by Dayton Ave. Tower in the early '80s, a recession time which contributed to the mass of stored diesels seen in the upper right background.

107

or that was matched up with the original outline, and as Los Angeles Basin took on the mantle of a huge megalopolis, the *ad hoc* solutions that kept Taylor Yard at least abreast of expanded train operations gave way to West Colton Yard.

There were moments, not infrequent, when two or three trains would be held out on the main at either end of Taylor, waiting perhaps hours just to get into its arrival tracks, partially because SP was busy, often because the yard was overflowing.

With West Colton confirmed in its dominant role in today's version of basin railroading, Taylor Yard has been left as a spawning ground for locals and industrial switchers. It also supports the Coast Line between Los Angeles and San Francisco, a route best described as moderately busy.

A heavy train of less-than-glamorous sugar beets slips down the Los Angeles river-bed just south of Taylor Yard. This was the second such train of the day; the first had preceded it up the coast by an hour.

Even coming off the Coast, many trains bypass the maze of terminal switches holding to the main line along San Fernando Road where crews are changed.

Of the two projects that went a long way toward reducing Taylor Yard's rank in town, the Palmdale Cut-off was first to come along. Actually it had been rumored for years that SP desired to join the Santa Fe-Union Pacific partnership in pushing its trains through short but steep gash in the San Gabriel mountain range, better known as Cajon Pass. That talk became three-dimensional reality in the late 1960s with a 78-mile extension that tied together two foot-of-the-mountain terminals at Bakersfield and Colton, creating a run that would see train crews crossing two of the West's most famous passes in a single lengthy assignment. There would be helpers, too, sometimes all the way, creating one of the longest regular tasks in this category as well.

Forty-six miles would be knocked off the route through Los Angeles in the process, and pressure upon Taylor Yard would be lessened for several years pending completion of a brand-new facility just west of Colton Tower's aging wooden structure.

As originally operated, the Colton Cut-off Line—as it was called by management—was operated by train orders sans block signals. A caboose was moved to Hiland, the peak of Cajon Pass, and was placed on a short piece of track where it went into action on a 24-hour basis as an open office. Eventually it was replaced by the current CTC installation with most sidings extended to a 1.7-mile gap between power switches. Since its opening, this line has seen a gradual expansion of traffic to the point where a typical day will generate a half dozen or so through movements of SP size, in a word, long and weighty.

The old way to the very industrious harbor district around Long Beach–San Pedro was by way of Taylor Yard's original centerpiece. As of late 1985 that emphasis had shifted eastwards to West Colton Yard. Transfer runs to UP or Santa Fe out of Dolores Yard (Harbor District base) now mostly cycle to West Colton, then on a mile or so to interchange by the old Colton Tower site. Still, the initial pathway remains with some locals shuttling between Taylor Yard and waterfront destinations.

South of Taylor, across from LAUPT's Mission Tower is the old coach yard, now a great intermodal center with a curiously named auxiliary yard, the Bullring, a bit off to the west near the local Chinatown. The whole creates an involved maze through which trains crawl their way in multiple directions.

Straight through from Bakersfield—in the instance of unit oil cuts to the Shell refinery—Harbor-bound trains flow through industrial sidings, past support or storage yards, mostly behind smaller units that are detailed on Espee's general roster of behemoths. SD and GP-9s beat a slow-paced tattoo across numerous switches and junctions, backed by that mainstay of any system terminal performance, EMD's SW-1500, of which this railroad holds title to a bundle. They seem to be everywhere there is a branch line and they are a multiplicity in the matrix.

Naturally there are plenty of six-motored units, too, their presence up on the point generally denoting a destination for some major point, Taylor or West Colton Yard outbound, Compton, Orange County, perhaps the Harbor District inbound.

As good as anywhere to focus upon Southern Pacific's empire within an empire is Mission Tower, the onetime epicenter of first-class transportation now more attuned to the raucous blast of freight unit air horns calling for this or that routing between those many destinations that span the Los Angeles Basin. A few hundred yards west of the stucco tower lies Los Angeles Union Station, its Amtrak schedules offering at least a modicum of past glory.

In spite of the downgrading of Taylor Yard, Southern Pacific in particular puts on a great show along the Los Angeles River. Rangy piggyback trains swing out from the loading center just to the east of Mission Tower, slipping up northward along the east bank past Taylor Yard, taking a right or left at outlying Burbank Tower to either Oakland or Portland's unloading cranes. Left here is coastal territory, the San Fernando Valley and a smell of salt spray for dozens of mileposts before reaching another great metropolitan port city slapped down on San Francisco Bay. Speed right past Burbank Junction, and as you pass Lockheed Aircraft's vast aviation complex you're bound for Tehachapi where shiny aluminum trailers circle continuously on this twisting access to the great Central Valley. Ahead then are several hundred miles of mostly tangent roadbed where friction, not climb, is all that matters and not much at that.

Triple-rigged diesel lashups can run in the highest notches from Bakersfield to Red Bluff, pausing quickly in Fresno and Roseville to bring fresh train crews aboard as normally it's a total scenario of "green pots" save for Amtrak's occasional impact.

Other trains come down the Los Angeles River from two directions, north or south, calling for a route to turn eastward, then a few hours later West Colton's retarders may be hacking them to pieces before remobilizing them to Kansas City, Memphis, East St. Louis or New Orleans. A train may fill at City of Industry, again at West Colton and then blast up a tricky, short hill beyond, emerging from Beaumont Pass to face varied types of desert for several hundred miles while carrying one of the many transcontinental symbols that confirm Espee as a long hauler.

There is, however, a bit of sideshow available past Mission Tower which proceeds via a unique routing out to El Monte. Utilizing an old Pacific Electric trail, the railroad constructed a bypass south of Los Angeles Division's main line between Pasadena Junction and El Monte. It splits the immensely busy San Bernardino Freeway right down its middle, rejoining mainline iron just short of City of Industry yard. It is labeled the State Street Line.

The harbor district of Los Angeles' terminal action is built upon a combination of onetime PE system blended with SP trackwork to form a local network that pokes into every nook and cranny of this continually expanding zone. Not too many years ago there was some unused acreage amidst the docks, oil refineries and warehouses that sprawl across many square miles stretching about Long Beach and San Pedro.

But no longer.

As trade with the Pacific Rim countries has expanded so has the importance of running diesels to meet ships at water's edge.

The docks have turned into a major supplier of complete trainloads for the land bridge, so called because it shortcuts transit through the Panama Canal for east-west global traffic by using U.S. transcontinentals. Espee is a major player in this carload producing game. Along with this concept the railroad added its personal engineering touch in a design of double-stacked cars which hold containers in a two-story arrangement. Many complete trains of such design are run in both directions between Southern California and New Orleans, Kansas City and East St. Louis.

There is a checkerboard option of train dispatching between major yards and the harbor. From emaciated Taylor Yard, it is a direct shot south by way of Mission Tower, then Los Angeles River's east bank to a crossing at Redondo Junction of the Santa Fe, after which rails funnel moves to trace a line down onetime PE trackage through Compton and into the port district.

A parallel course exists down Alameda Street, the original way to dockside before electric trains ceased their operations. The bulk of maritime business is geared to an east-west trend line, so with Taylor Yard being downgraded in favor of West Colton's modern yard, the way east and south of downtown Los Angeles is the principal one. There are two possibilities, both depending heavily upon ex-PE lines.

One trails along the Santa Ana branch from Firestone Park; it turns north at Studebaker to Los Nietos, thence to Bartolo and City of Industry (on UP rails), while the other is placed a bit further north beginning at Slauson Junction. Then it too picks its way through suburbia to Los Nietos, which sits almost astride Santa Fe's Los Angeles Division main line.

Peripheral action around the Basin is drama in its own right. Every access to SP's Southern California domain involves some variation of a mountain pass, implying that helpers are commonplace, which is true. Within a relatively short span of mileposts, the coastal plain gives way to a ring of tall mountains which hem in the Basin from three sides, directions taken by SP trains. Only the southern exit to San Diego isn't blocked by a mountain, and Espee doesn't go that way.

An American President Lines stack train crawls through Dolores Yard with a pure set of GP40Xs doing the honors.

The other two local major lines, Santa Fe and Union Pacific, generally don't couple extra power to their movements. Instead, they tailor tonnage to horsepower combinations on the point, while SP's concern for heavy trains leads to different presumptions. Consequently, more heavy-duty six-axled power is found sitting on departure tracks in Espee terminals than is average elsewhere.

Currently, the east end, Cajon Pass and Beaumont Pass, reflect most helper demands, essentially because the Palmdale Cut-off reduced train movements through Soledad Canyon, and the ascent there is fairly modest. The west end routing to San Francisco is a more normal type railroad, save for a brief fling with hills west of the San Fernando Valley. Booster power, however, is commonplace on the Los Angeles–San Francisco run for a short segment where Cuesta grade is encountered at San Luis Obispo, half-way up the coast.

Heading eastward from West Colton, the line quickly crosses Santa Fe's main line, the Third Subdivision, at a high-speed crossing where UP trains also stride by way of trackage rights. Then it passes through old Colton Yard, now merely a set of storage rails, and reaches into a narrow canyon for 15 miles' worth of upgrade that climbs along for just under 2% through San Timeteo Canyon. Not all eastbounds call for helpers, as the frequent, solid piggyback trains are fairly light despite their elongated profiles. Extra help up Beaumont Pass may be tied in right out of the yard, or, as is more common, added at Loma Linda X-overs a couple miles east of the Santa Fe crossing. There are usually a couple of helper sets working

112

the pass on each shift, floating back and forth on both sides of the hill, particularly on the longer run west out of Indio. Gradient there is basically the same as that east of West Colton Yard, though substantially longer, requiring a longer period to surmount. So even lighter movements, especially hotshots like the BSM, will be aided through Garnet and Palm Springs westward to the crest.

In tackling Cajon Pass, SP, unlike the other two carriers which use its narrow access to the high desert, typically adds on helpers. Frequently they stay on from end to end so they can conquer Tehachapi as well. Over the years, it is interesting to watch how opinions have changed about extra motive power, though much of it has derived from a synthesis of high-horsepower designs with short, speedy trains to meet truck competition.

At one period, the rear end, single unit seems in favor on SP; at other moments, a mid-train positioning of several big ones is in vogue on heavier trains despite up to six units on the point. Clearly tonnage is a factor, but

Working Long Beach Yard, a duo of SW-1500s pushes a long tank into a yard track before grabbing a cut of cars and taking off for San Pedro.

within that framework a bit of modification has been in order over the years since 1,500-hp F units put in an appearance.

Opinions as to motive power requirements parallel the changing nature of rolling stock that leads to different weight distribution from engine to caboose or "end of train" as the present is termed. The dynamics of container cars and hi-cube boxcars affect placement of helpers in each train they are coupled to.

Nowhere in this complex rail matrix, which is Southern Pacific from Colton west to the sea, is the meaning of Pacific Electric more important than in Orange County. In measuring growth that has brought trainload after trainload of loads onto SP roadbed no district has relied more upon its ex-juice line heritage than those connections which lie south of City of Industry and Los Nietos yards.

The principal routings out of the City of Industry Yard inbound are through Los Nietos, using Union Pacific main for a while, switching back to home road rails and then physically crossing the Santa Fe main at grade with Los Nietos yard nearby. Los Nietos spills out to a junction at Studebaker, harbor traffic turning west here, Orange County trains southeast.

In 1958 the Santa Ana branch was not far removed from being an interurban line, handling 15,910 annual carloadings that year. By the early 1980s it was producing a statistic that exceeded 58,500, a regular "Mother Lode" of carloadings. As Orange County's multiple branch lines have leaped into prominence, the number of trains and switch engine assignments have kept pace. A typical day will see three or four good-sized trains connecting the many sidings and industrial servicing yards with City of Industry and eventually West Colton. A dozen daily switching tricks are routine, Geeps and SW-1500s poking in and out of a myriad of stub tracks, mostly in a trade involving food products, paper products and basic chemicals. There are heavier trains in than out, the ratio running to nine loads arriving for every load shipped out.

Fifty miles due east of downtown Los Angeles is the operational center, the hub not only of Southern California but for hundreds of Southern Pacific miles east or west. Quite simply the railroad had outgrown its longtime local nerve center in Taylor Yard, and the emphasis on business was shifting south to the harbor and toward Orange County. Taylor no longer was an axis around which train action revolved. For the increasing traffic that was heading east, SP reacted by creating West Colton Yard.

A colorful symbolism of electronics, buttons, dials and cathode ray tubes dominate the control functions of a physical creature that extends for six miles. A central classification yard consists of 48 tracks capable of holding 2,800 cars, while an eight-track west end receiving yard is geared to hold 1,400 cars. Departures move from the east end, 14 tracks and 2,000 cars of capacity.

A busy shuttle service exists to all points west: Santa Ana Branch,

In the mid-1960s a switcher and caboose head out of El Centro, California, bound for trackage on the Holton Interurban, part of the gathering network in the Imperial Valley.

the Harbor District, City of Industry, literally dozens of locations. Arriving from that direction unorganized, long chains of cars are forced over the crest by pairs of permanently assigned SD-38s in the 2970 class, purchased exclusively for gravity yard service. Other two- and three-unit lashups, usually brought together on a more *ad hoc* basis, clean the classification tracks, dragging fully blocked cuts out to the departure yard to await arrival of road power. Quite a few trains, concentrated mainly in the piggyback/container trade, have no use for classification, but may fill out at West Colton. These runs originating at the downtown Los Angeles intermodal terminal, or from Valla, an exclusive trailer/container terminal near Los Nietos and from Dolores Yard in the harbor district, are already blocked. Running around the yard on high iron, they pause briefly for fresh crews, possibly fill.

Seasonal patterns, tonnage flows that shift direction on a day-to-day basis affect the tempo of West Colton. A good average would put 50 to 70 inbound and outbound trains through on a 2400 clock. The crest can handle six to eight cars a minute, roughly double that of older retarder-equipped yards. The large engine servicing bay will be handling 80 to 100 units a day, servicing them, perhaps altering their makeup, then lining them on the ready tracks for outbound runs. With so much motive power passing through, the yard needs a specialized post, a crest herder, to direct diesels, with a minimum of delay to all concerned.

A balloon track exists at the yard's east perimeter; its entry switch leads from one leg of a heavy-duty wye that provides access to Cajon Pass and the Palmdale Cut-off, an extremely important connection. A second wye, this one buried in the yard, caters to the diesel servicing department.

Round-the-clock railroading is a much abused term. Here at West Colton Yard and throughout the matrix in general it's full of real meaning.

115

Just east of Colton the 8338 powers a westbound freight past the lead engine—8531— of a helper set waiting to assist the next freight up through Beaumont Pass.

A big GE unit powers a westbound past the somewhat beat-up image of Colton Tower.

Opposite: While the window has disappeared from the *Sunset Limited's* rear, SP at least provided a neon I.D. for the train, shown during a stop at Colton station.

One of the early U33-Cs leads an eastbound train through Garnet Siding at the foot of Beaumont Pass. Despite hundreds of miles of desert main there are relatively few spots that expose SP roadbed and trains to such naked sand as the area immediately west of Indio.

Bought originally for ore train service over Beaumont Pass the U28C operated almost exclusively in Southern California territory for many years. Here, two are seen sweating their way up Beaumont Pass near Palm Springs on a hot summer day.

The long-rumored Palmdale Cut-off line was ultimately to become a part of Cajon Pass, putting SP trains in the same area as the famous "Sullivan's Curve." Now on a single assignment, engine crews would work two of railroading's most famous passes, Cajon and Tehachapi.

No matter from what angle, SP trackage into Southern California either enters via a pass or a tunnel. In this case it's little known Soledad Canyon, which plays second fiddle to the Palmdale Cut-off.

ABOUT THOSE DIESELS

SP was a seller's market

A N OFT HEARD LAMENT about the early stages of dieselization was, "They're all alike, products of an assembly line mentality." For a time those who expressed and repeated this phrase, mainly steam locomotive enthusiasts, appeared to be right. EMD's blunt-nosed cabs, FTs, F-3s and F-7s appeared to be taking over the rail world, validating mass production techniques, flooding new diesel shops and ready tracks from Maine to California.

"Who needs boiler makers? We want electricians!" sang the employment ads of the late '40s and early '50s.

Southern Pacific threatened to emulate every other major railroad with the arrival of black and silver cabs by the hundreds. Anywhere you looked, East St. Louis, Houston, Tehachapi, the Cascades, the head end was uniformly dominated by Fs, conjuring visions of a totally monolithic roster when the last steam boiler turned cold. Other than switchers, the soothsayers seemed to have confirmed their calling.

Two circumstances combined to prevent that happening on Southern Pacific—even in the 1980s—though the cry about standardization is again heard in contemporary bull sessions. First, locomotive manufacturers responded to competitive pressures year after year. EMD so dominated things that it fielded new models to render obsolete the existing—the favorite philosophy of parent General Motors concerning automobiles. The smaller makers, Alco, Baldwin, Lima-Hamilton, even Fairbanks-Morse, were so overwhelmed by EMD that one obvious way to stimulate sales was a new product line.

Secondly, SP's motive power people displayed a willingness to sample, an attitude that led to small numbers of many locomotive models. Manufacturers were eager to try their products on a Southern Pacific division because if it worked well along the fringes of the 15,000-square-mile Mojave Desert or bested the worst the tortuous Sierra or Cascades

Opposite: Hard to believe but Southern Pacific did wash its engines in earlier years. Just in from New Orleans with the *Sunset Limited* this trio of Alco PAs has just been through the laundry at Taylor Yard.

121

could throw at tonnage then, hell, it would work anywhere. Carrying a Southern Pacific endorsement into a Norfolk and Western or a New York Central purchasing department was a symbol of success.

As the diesel era matured, emphasis evolved from just having them to a horsepower race. Brute strength was what counted. Manufacturers barely had filled their order books with one model when another of superior physique was penciled in on the drawing boards, sometimes because of engineering or mechanical flaws discovered on the previous model. No longer pampered by the research boys, diesels now subjected to daily pounding and the strain and shock of hauling thousands of tons unobserved, failed in ways, often minor, occasionally major, that designers never contemplated.

When too many complaints were heard, just tell 'em the new model due out soon will lick the problems. This led to periodic showings of demonstrators. On SP this meant your latest example was a bit at risk, for its decision makers always want to know how much a unit can haul, not necessarily how fast it is, or other niceties.

One day the author was following a set of four Alco DL-721 demonstrators south out of Santa Barbara on the Coast Line. As usual, Espee had tied as much tonnage to their tail as possible, plus some. The Alco engineering rep was riding in the last cab, and having talked with him the day before, we were aware of his opinion about what the good ol' SP usually did to demos. Having taken the hole at Seacliff siding for the San Francisco-bound *Daylight,* the snow-white foursome of high-nosed units was ready to leave. As with all Schenectady-built diesels, the smoke came first, clouds of it.

Nothing moved.

So the hogger just opened the throttle wider. Again no forward progress. The four units just sat there, literally shaking themselves into a breakdown as they stalled wide open. Meantime, the Alco rep came boiling out of the rear cab on the run, literally flying across the intervening units to reach the first. One can only imagine what he said, but it probably was "expletive deleted" as he shoved the SP engineer aside, taking charge.

On another occasion, the much-ballyhooed arrival of the initial German-built diesel-hydraulics offered minor evidence of continental differences in railroading. Just off the boat in Houston, the first four-unit set had stopped at Colton on its way to the Sacramento General Shop for many items peculiar to the SP system. Already, a bracket holding the obligatory rerailing frog had broken, leading a carman with a portable welding machine to attempt repairs. One of the Germans who accompanied the units came over to engage in conversation. In very good English he unloaded his first impressions of Southern Pacific technique, which, it must be said, were hardly praiseworthy. The gist of it was that he had a hard time fathoming U.S. procedures; in Germany locomotives were run

German technology, American erecting shops. Fresh from Alco a trio of U.S.-built diesel-hydraulics pulls away on the eastern slope of Beaumont Pass as SP experimented with an alternative to the oftentimes electrical problems that plagued first-generation examples of diesel-electrics.

perhaps 200–300 miles at most, pulled off and serviced for hours, and, yes, even washed.

After several months of Southern Pacific experiences, of motive power assigned to a train for 1,000–1,500 miles at a crack, only to be returned home a short time later, the German technician arrived back home with a different book of railroad stories.

To a degree, SP's mechanical department became a sort of postwar Altoona of western lines. No other carrier was as willing to experiment or bring forth new ideas, or to try state-of-the-art motive power as the San Francisco-based one was. It took the lead in evaluating diesel-hydraulics, even going so far as to have Alco manufacture a type to U.S. standards. Dissatisfied with the electrical performance of the standard diesel-electric unit of the time, the railroad's look at Krauss-Maffei technology sought alternatives to a motor drive. If nothing else, the move spurred domestic builders to focus more effort upon that part of locomotive reliability, a trend that continues in the present. There were double-engined freight units on SP, too, not that it took a lead in this category. Union Pacific did. Still, the DD-35s and U-50s were represented on a roster, if only as a trial size.

The 1970s were the heyday of diversity on a Southern Pacific locomotive roster. A tremendous amount of first- and second-generation power rolled over the mountains and plains, switched Pacific Coast harbors and was repaired at Sacramento Shops, at Eugene, Los Angeles, Houston, Pine Bluff or several lesser spots. It was a time when six-motored units were delivered from both EMD and General Electric by the hundreds. Yet for all that, rarities abounded. Alco C-415s could be spotted in a Los Angeles area yard, a few Century six-motored units were in road service up north,

Fairbanks-Morse Trainmasters were kept busy in the commute trade handling 1920s Harriman coaches, while the maze of system branch lines were and still are host to early-generation road switchers. Their modest weight and horsepower still make them efficient, and so they get rebuilt, as no one wants to put an almost million-dollar engine in part-time service these days.

Among the 2,400 or so units that have been the average SP roster for many years there have always been a few units of just about anything a builder turned out from the late 1950s on. The six-axled type, SD-40s, SD-45s and their tunnel motor variants, along with U30Cs and U33Cs, totally saturated the mainline brigade in that epoch.

Within the framework, there were small orders of types for specialized needs. The 5300-series SD-39s were almost exclusive Southern California property, assigned mostly Bakersfield-Los Angeles, as were 10 U28-Cs numbered 7150–7159, plus the 7900 series of U30Cs, which ran to 37 units total. If there was a particular need, a unique bit of landform somewhere on its wide-flung system, SP seemed willing to buy tailor-made locomotives for the purpose. Standardization in the sense that many large railroads perceive it was not and is not a Southern Pacific discipline.

Tunnel motors were conceived to SP specs, customized for high-altitude ops with numerous tunnels, generating a need for a better breathing diesel on western divisions, hence the SD-40T and its slightly more powerful brother, the SD-45T. Outside of Rio Grande, nowhere else does this see-through profile railroad. As matters now stand they are no longer a western lines exclusive. Low-grilled units are mainline SP, East St. Louis and New Orleans to anywhere west the rail is heavy enough. With run-throughs it also implies many places east as well.

Among other variants pounding down the rails are long-nosed SD40T-2s rigged for a master-mate relationship as radio-controlled helpers. Again willing to experiment, the SP apparently found the idea wanting, not really a viable alternative for the likes of a Tehachapi or the Cascades where steep slopes and numerous tunnels interfere with radio transmissions. Last seen on an occasional heavy train on the Alturas Line as home base for the dual setup, the concept has faded.

Changing times, changing ideas. No longer is a six-axled locomotive the darling at Southern Pacific. Emerging from the late '70s and early '80s recession with a reduced financial base, the railroad has not been ordering new power with the same abandon it exhibited in prior years. Concurrently, emphasis has shifted to four-motored types; GP40-2s and B30-7s have emerged as the domineering types selected. The early SD-45s have been rebuilt, over 150 of them at Sacramento General shops by the mid-'80s. Not only gutted to the frame while being resurrected they have been derated to 3,200 horsepower and designated SD-45R (rebuild). The 20-cylinder engine common to SD-45s runs cooler, gets better fuel effi-

In a demonstration of poor combustion a U33C muscles its way through Cliff Siding in the Tehachapi Mountains. By 1987 most of these units were gone or sitting on dead lines from Los Angeles to Pine Bluff.

ciency, lasts longer at the reduced rating, making it comparable in performance to the 16-cylinder prime mover that comes fitted to a GP-40. Meanwhile, pug-nosed ''C'' models of U28, U30 and U33 have been traded into General Electric for a large batch of B30-7s in the 7700 and 7800 series. That builder's presence now rides on four-axle trucks.

By comparison with their EMD counterparts, the C-C marks from GE haven't fared that well. Coming along four to five years later than the early SD-45s, the U-33Cs of the 8600–8700 grouping were sidelined for years prior to being traded in. On a lengthy trip during mid-'86 only a single U-33C was seen working. Outwardly in terrible physical shape, it was idling in a set of mixed B-B power at Pine Bluff Yard. A few others were seen being towed dead in a train or rusting at San Antonio and Houston.

Check out the major western railroads today. Burlington Northern, Union Pacific, and the Santa Fe are engaged in pruning their rosters to a few models. It is certainly sensible to standardize, easier on maintenance forces, with fewer spare parts to stock and other benefits. Southern Pacific seems to be considering the trend, though whatever the future brings, it is going to take a lot longer, since there is a lot further to go. With the Santa Fe merger rejected and its claim of financial trauma, SP may have to rethink: new or rebuilt?

As you review literature about diesel locomotive production of this or that prototype from Fs to the latest example of a builder's erecting shop, check out the roads that bought, and notice how many times ''Southern Pacific'' appears in the list. That idea extends right down into the 1980s.

Electro-Motive is now engaged in an extended proof-of-concept testing of its GP-60s series on western railroads. They recently showed off for a few trips on Santa Fe, then will be consigned to SP for a full year.

Locomotives are demonstrated on many railroads, they get blooded on Southern Pacific.

125

On its way to Bakersfield the 801 makes a modest step upwards through Soledad Canyon before arriving at the heavy hill, Tehachapi.

Working as a helper, a set of Fs pushes hard against the Sierra Nevada monolith on its way east with a reefer train.

While the valley below is sweltering, a four-unit set of Fs climbs up the west side of the Sierra on its way to Sparks, Nev. The cut of cattle cars behind the engine is a reminder of how far back this photo was—1964.

During the 1960s Cotton Belt engines didn't routinely stray across the entire system as they do today. The 949 pretty much stayed at home, seldom getting to the West Coast. It is shown on the ready track at East St. Louis, Illinois.

Another era finds a blunt-nosed Alco PA leading the *Lark* on its overnight run between Los Angeles and San Francisco. Boeing and its 707 were at least five years away from reality at this moment on the Coast Line when train order offices kept faith with trains that passed in the night.

In a smooth grey coat that was to last well into the charter years of Amtrak, the 6198 idles in the outside service bay beside Taylor Yard's diesel shop.

Fresh in the black and silver tones and already doing yeoman chores in road service, a set of early-generation, six-motored SDs descends through Soledad Canyon near Los Angeles. Number boards and freight designations such as #804 work to the tune of dynamic brakes on a downgrade.

An all-Alco performance in the early 1950s powers the southbound *San Joaquin Daylight* through the sharp U-turn at Caliente.

Other than the Loop itself, probably the most famous feature of the Tehachapi area is the great U curve at Caliente where the line turns upon itself. A group of RSD-15s is seen making that turn on its way downhill to Bakersfield.

Perhaps the briefest of all Alcos on Southern Pacific were the rather ugly center-cab C-415 models. These two are shown working the City of Industry Yard.

Strange looking things in Southern California! Just in off the boat from Houston, Texas, the initial westbound run of KM diesel-hydraulics speeds through Ontario, California, the company dynamometer car tucked on behind to get an initial reaction to their performance.

Among the many unique locomotives acquired and tried by SP was a four-unit set of Swiss-engined U25B rebuilds outshopped by Morrison-Knudsen in 1978. They're shown here on the dead line at Eugene, Oregon, in 1985.

DESERT CORRIDOR

Busiest division on the SP

TUCSON DIVISION IS Southern Pacific's hottest property in terms of both train action and geography. Along several hundred mileposts of main line and branches, the landscape is the same: desert. Tucumcari, El Paso, Yuma and all the other places on this extensive division have one thing in common, their city limits fade abruptly into dry washes, scrub brush and expansive horizons that feature endless peaks to the furthest perimeter. It is a physical domain of dust, heat and great, blue, often cloud-studded skies that overlook a most explosive brand of single-track railroading.

East beyond El Paso, and west of Yuma, there are alternative routes over which trains can perform, but if it's the long-distance type of carloading, and if it's moving by way of SP, it must polish the welded rail of Tucson Division's pressure cooker.

Intriguingly, much of Tucson Division performs at high altitude. It crosses the Continental Divide at one point, and the second highest point on SP is not an Oregon mountaintop but on the dry desert south of Tucumcari, New Mexico. It features a subdivision east of Tucson which, though desert in manner, is known among operating crews as "Old Stormy" because of its late summer rainfall when arid landscapes can be turned into raging deluges just like that. This moniker is hard to imagine on a day when direct line of sight extends for a dozen mileposts under a sterling clear sky. But the cautionary title is earned.

Things are not always as they seem on the desert. Those in intimate contact with its often petulant moods, as railroaders must be, come to expect and plan for a few uncommon events sandwiched in among the otherwise routine passage of trains across the Sonoran Desert which makes up southern Arizona and New Mexico.

Moderately far away to the north, Santa Fe gallops across these same two states on its twin-tracked high iron, owning a clear-cut advantage

Opposite: More often than not, a midsummer afternoon on SP's southern Arizona trail will mean a sky full of cumulous clouds, often bringing torrents of brief rain, enough in fact to give the line east of Tucson a nickname, "Old Stormy." Two GP-40s head into Tucson, passing Dragoon in the process.

133

because it is basically a line without sidings. Modern operating techniques based upon bidirectional running funnel trains from side to side with little reference to predominate direction, since only track occupancy between high-speed crossovers is relevant. Moreover, with the almost total disappearance of any kind of passenger trains from its timetables, the coddling once demanded by a *Super Chief* can be reserved for a new star, the TOFC/COFC run.

Southern Pacific, on the other hand, is first and foremost a single-track railroad, primarily guided by systemwide reliance upon centralized traffic control. Nowhere is this so needed as on Tucson Division, which must create a contemporary, competitive answer from the rash of trains descending upon it by way of Los Angeles Division to the west, and Kansas City and San Antonio Divisions from the east.

Light rail and unkempt roadbed force Tucson Division timetable instructions to keep all six-axled power off the branches unless special permission is obtained. The prohibition results in scenes like this where seven GP-35s are used to power the Clifton Branch copper train.

134

In recent years much has been made of contrasting ideas on train handling between SP and its major western rail rivals, Santa Fe and Union Pacific. The latter have significant portions of double-tracked line in their trunk routes to impact a trend toward high-speed, short and modest tonnage haulers. This of course fits the trailer train scenario exceptionally well. SP, by contrast, is sometimes condescendingly put down for its philosophy of long, heavy trains with an implied handicap in performance. Short trains on single track, even with CTC, will require more meets, more siding time.

To critics of the long train, an example of getting the utmost from signaling, motive power and speed is run off on the 560 miles between two river boundaries, the Colorado on the west and Rio Grande on the east. The defense rests upon a study of Tucson Division's train handling.

Sitting in on a dispatcher's CTC panel, no matter upon what railroad, one is quite naturally struck by a sanitized, almost dimensionless presentation. Utterly straight lines, occasionally relieved by an angle, portray the up and down, the curvature, and the audible feelings of real life out there on the main. Colored lights and siding symbols provide a graphic representation of how to get from Point A to Point B in the swiftest of times, along with a minute by minute history of when it was accomplished. The modern world of railroading is like that, now that train orders and chess-like moves of handwritten or typed upon "flimsies" are becoming passe. So much so on Southern Pacific that radio dispatching geared to "block times" is now predominant in non-CTC territory, as trains are simply given exclusive right to occupy a space between siding limits or across many siding segments as traffic dictates.

What train orders there are come from copy machines rather than typewriters, concerned principally with such matters as slow orders rather than meets, for the DTC system is more flexible on that score. Besides, the "TO OP" has joined the ranks of extinct species on many railroads, including Espee. Very few places exist where orders can be picked up except at terminals.

It is definitely impractical to cast any particular railroad segment in terms of train movements by the numbers, at least for more than a short time. Certainly the main line, Yuma to El Paso, will probably have more action than Roseville–Ogden, founded upon population distribution, a desire to keep as much revenue in hand as possible, and so forth. But just how many will that be in precise train movements?

From year to year traffic sources, the economy, events, annual seasons cause considerable deviations on train sheets. Still, for Tucson Division the peak periods have been logged at 28 to 40 trains in a 24-hour span. Considering its single-track character, the electronic commands must have been active on the CTC system, since there are few rusty sidings anywhere.

Cloned! That perhaps is an appropriate account of sidings that stretch from El Paso west to Yuma or northeast to Tucumcari. For it is a visual fact that desert passing tracks seemed to be formed from a common visual mold. Where CTC is in place from Yuma to El Paso standard siding length extends between eight and nine thousand feet, a dimension that is being strained by today's lengthier trains. When remote-controlled sidings were first placed in service during the early days of dieselization there was plenty of room for a moving meet, or "slider," with some room to spare, but today's longer movements are often crowding both siding switches. As a result, the advertising department's boast about nonstop encounters is not all that common an event.

On the average there is a siding every six to nine miles from end to end on 560 miles' worth of east-west trunk railroad across the southwest desert, barring a few odds and ends of double track, most notable of which extends for 30 some miles on the east of Tucson out to Mescal.

Fundamentally they exhibit little individualism from place to place. Mohawk siding in Arizona portrays the personality of Dona siding east of Deming, New Mexico, though they come separated by 444 mileposts' worth of steel rail. Each sits upon a dusty desert bed with mountains filling the distant horizon. Each has the single lens searchlight signal with its "A" panel (forbidding a train to pass its limits while awarding main line or siding as a dispatcher dictates). Both show off well-polished rail.

Yet for all their similarities, a hogger or dispatcher could quickly point out subtle differences that must be considered when trains meet one another. A bit of upgrade on canted roadbed at Steins siding requires different handling than a straight forward entrance to Casa Grande, for instance. Little details like that plus train handling characteristics, the amount of horsepower per ton or weather conditions may mean an ability to shave moments off a meet. Where you allow two minutes for a train to get into one siding, it might take three or four at another location further on. "Look-alike" does not mean either monotonous or standardized when it comes to moving tonnage across Tucson's two busiest subdivisions, the Gila and Lordsburg. The former links Tucson with Yuma, the latter links Tucson with El Paso.

The division has two other major subs. The Phoenix, which courses over 208 parallel miles north of the Gila Subdivision while beginning and ending on it, and the Carrizozo Sub, which is newly upgraded on its 331-mile reach, more important now with the acquisition of ex-Rock Island trackage into Kansas City.

Added to this far-flung reach is a core pattern of branch lines which throb to the beat of copper mining, an industry not exactly robust in the 1980s. While branch lines have pretty much fallen into disfavor among railroads in modern times, SP has long worked a minor network of them around its geographical center across the southwest desert.

136

"Copper Circle" is an imaginary 125-mile radius drawn upon an Arizona map, with its center at Tucson Yard. An area which until a few years ago produced a goodly portion of the nation's copper, it has since fallen upon hard times for a variety of reasons including foreign source competition and the environmental movement. Many mines have been closed either on a permanent basis or until economic forces look better. Some still produce, and the trick is to mine copper profitably.

Despite many closures, there's a fair amount of localized train action on both branch and main line for shippers with names like Phelps-Dodge and Kennecott Corporation. It's an aspect of this diversified railroad involving rolling stock rarely seen outside the area or off Tucson Division's steel.

Centered to an extent upon the terminal at Tucson, action takes place especially on the Clifton and Hayden Branches with lesser exertions on the Douglas and Globe-Miami lines, the latter of which has recently been proposed for abandonment. Also, the Nogales Branch south out of Tucson is both a source of copper in past years and a connection with Mexico's rail system. Most of these branches retain some vestige of past or hoped-for carloadings.

In this "circle" is a small roster of specialized cars and motive power not seen far afield. Today's copper ore is fairly low grade, requiring an amount of processing, primarily crushing, to obtain a powderlike concentrate which is then supplied to a nearby smelter or, in some instances, carried by railcar from more remote sources. Two branches, descriptions of which follow, provide an insight into what this business is like as it complements mainline handiwork in the region. One illustrates copper ore haulage, the other how concentrate keeps trains on the callboard.

On the Hayden Branch, SP hauls 100-ton loads of ore in cars provided by a copper firm. On the Clifton Branch it utilizes its own rolling stock to bring in white powdered concentrate to a smelter. The material is hauled in bottom dump gons with 100-ton capacity, often seen trailing along in the consists of both branch runs and mainline trains, as well. Another style of regional equipment is a flatcar equipped with crosswise racks, specially constructed to haul copper anode in 700-pound slabs from smelter to refinery, the final step in a complex process of turning ore into finished metal.

Although copper is a significant sideshow on Tucson Division, it is usually overshadowed by mainline craftsmanship.

The Hayden Branch comes first.

Most days a mainline freight circulates both ways between Tucson and Hayden by way of the Gila and Phoenix subdivisions to Magma, Arizona, thence over 51 miles of light rail, the Hayden Branch. There is a rule on this division that all but four-axled locomotives stay off branch lines and it has provided the local scene with motive power not commonplace elsewhere. The 6300 series of GP-35s has been concentrated on this division, up to seven of them at a time heading up branch-line runs while the so-called TEBUs, two GP-40s and a booster are frequently seen as well.

Standing for Tractive Effort Booster Units, the acronym TEBU was turned out of the Sacramento General Shops to handle extra heavy loads at speeds less than 25 mph. Ore certainly fits that concept. A dozen such units were produced from retired U25Bs and they have neither cab nor prime mover. Filled with 37 tons of concrete to bring their weight up to 280,000 pounds, they are connected to a GP40-2 at either end and operated as a semi-permanently connected three-unit locomotive. Equipped with traction motors that draw from the powered units, they also hold a 2,800-gallon fuel tank which connects to the GP40-2s, extending their range. The only other place these units work is in Oregon, on the Toledo Branch.

Getting back to the Hayden Branch, it's the final 12 miles that exist between a cactus-studded link with Kennecott Copper Company at Ray Jct. and Hayden that another of SP's more unusual enterprises is generated. Between Ray Jct. and Winkleman—a point just east of Hayden— 24-hour-a-day operations put the railroad in the ore hauling business in a big way, even in 1986. As previously mentioned, the plight of the copper industry has been well publicized, but it's not totally negative with a couple of those huge open-pit mines still functioning including Kennecott's Ray Mines Division.

Southern Pacific provides a tie-in between the multicolored slopes of the pit and a smelter at Winkleman, hauling ore around the clock.

There's little between Tucson, Ariz., and Nogales except a long, barren track, but the SP keeps a solo 4400 in Nogales to handle the detail of exchange between it and traffic coming from Mexico.

One of the more unusual features of SP's Arizona–New Mexico territory is the survival of a few old coaling towers from steam engine days. Here, a rebuilt GP-35 drifts by one of those towers near Benson, Arizona.

Initially Kennecott provides the first few miles of the journey, connecting the pit area to Ray Jct. with its own brightly painted GP39s toting perhaps 50 to 55 heavily topped-off cars to a meeting with red and grey units at the junction. In a well-coordinated routine move, the big road leaves a set of empties while picking up loads. Then crews of both trains head out in opposite directions, to meet on the next go-around in roughly three hours.

Apparently the copper firm has long-range plans for its ore cars; roller-bearinged and of recent design they bear builders' plates of 1984 and '85 vintage, hardly a type of investment one expects of short-term schemes.

SP provides the midpoint in this process, exchanging loads and empties, forwarding modern cars to Winkleman where their heavy loads are dumped upon a conveyor belt for a short move uphill to a smelter. In early 1986 both railroads were scheduling six round trippers every 24 hours, utilizing two crews on 12-hour assignments. The ore cars initialed with KCC reporting marks average between 180,000 to 200,000-pound capacity so with a trainload of 50 to 55 cars the gross would be above 6,000 tons, enough to require five to six units of four-motored locomotives.

How then can Kennecott get away with only two units? The answer is obviously gradient. The copper company's rail line runs downhill, so it basically needs only braking power on loads. SP's chore is an uphill run, requiring a much greater effort, hence the larger locomotive set.

139

Just getting to Ray Jct. from the connection with mainline iron at Magma is itself a bit unique. Roadbed extends through several miles of tight rock cliffs, trailing along the precipitous course of the Gila River. Restricted to alternating zones of 10 and 20-mph territory, track pierces three tunnels and mentions 14 places where side clearances are less than standard from MP 971.8 to MP 992.3, the latter being just short of where rails emerge into a narrow valley by Ray Jct. A round-tripper as previously mentioned connects Tucson and copper-smelting plants with such things as sulphuric acid, timber and bulk chemicals, not only to Kennecott but to the San Manuel Railroad as well. That line comes in just east of Winkelman, providing another smelter at San Manuel with access to the outside rail world.

The daily hauler from Tucson provides raw materials for both smelters and in return lugs their product out. It is a pretty fair-sized run in both directions with the crew laying over in Hayden before a return to Tucson's important terminal.

An additional aspect of Hayden is the so-called "yard goat," a concoction made up of mainline power profiles that most railroads would have a hard time defining as such. With copper processing being a continuous process that eats up a lot of materials besides ore, the smelter at Winkleman requires many carloads daily.

Hayden Yard is situated on a slight incline with a track leading from the east end to the smelting plant, several hundred feet higher. By the time four heavy-duty units—the switcher—have spent a couple of hours assembling cars in their proper order, they may have anywhere from 60 to 70 loads to shove up a steep, two-mile spur. Clearly beyond the capability of small units, the necessity of large units in this setting is evident.

Hayden is intrinsically an end-of-branch location, yet there are times when three lashups of heavy-duty locomotive crowd the abbreviated, oil-stained fueling track. These include the daily train from Tucson, the four from the yard trick that is only on duty part time plus the ore hauler. Frequently the crew with a Kennecott schedule drops off for "beans," leaving the loads on a through track, while cutting power off to have it serviced during the break.

Sure, the Hayden Branch is just what its name implies. But it is untypical, even for Southern Pacific.

Clifton, Arizona, by highway, is reasonably close to Hayden. By railroad the two towns, both copper places, are 290 mileposts away from each other.

Most mornings the Clifton Turn is being assembled on Lordsburg's yard tracks to an accompaniment of main stem action. While "authorized freights," SP's lexicon for hotshots such as the BSM or the LAEST (Los Angeles to East St. Louis Trailers), come parading through town for a brief crew change, six or seven 6300-class units are gathering together some

The Hayden Yard Goat—all four units of it—pushes about 60 cars up the hill to the Kennecott smelter at Hayden, Arizona. Ore is dumped at a lower level and moved via conveyor belt to the smelter.

empty ore cars, tanks full of acid, other cars with copper concentrates and other open top hoppers with chemicals for the Phelps-Dodge smelter at the conclusion of the Clifton Branch, 70 miles northwest. Odds are these units have come over last night from Tucson, powering a daily drag that runs between the two division terminals. The units have been shut down for fuel conservation, so one by one an engineman cranks them to life, hovering a bit over each one to ensure performance. Then he returns to the lead unit.

As the local is attached to its caboose, a complete trailer-auto rack movement is roaring into action on an adjacent track. Slowly at first, then with increasing haste it accelerates, a mild scent of burnt diesel from a half-dozen road units blending with that of the four-axled kind, just as branch-line railroading shades into that of the main.

The Clifton-bound 6300s will be nosing out of Lordsburg while the hotshot is already two sidings east, straining to use every bit of horsepower it has coupled together, not so much because of weight but to make time.

Getting to Clifton and back to home base takes just about all the time the hours-of-service law allows. First comes the chore of putting a train together from several cuts. That takes a half hour or so. Then it is off on

Having delivered its train to Phelps-Dodge in Clifton, the branch-line turn is heading back for Lordsburg behind a roster of seven 6300-series GP-35s.

the branch with its deceptively maximum pace of 40 mph. However, on close inspection this branch contains many restrictions. There is a 24-mile section where 20 mph is the maximum, and 19 miles of 30-mph traveling. A 10-mph limit on about 15 miles hits hard because the last 13 miles into Clifton is at the lowest speed. Light, twisting iron caters to the very wandering course of the Gila River.

Nor is the line flat, especially for the initial 20 miles out of the originating yard, for there is a moderate upgrade run to Summit, 19 miles away from the main line. Generally unpopulated desert and range land, this area lies east of the parallel Peloncillo Mountains. After topping out, the rails follow a sloping 19 miles into Duncan where the line enters a shallow canyon carved out eons ago by the Gila River. Following along for several miles at very low speed the turn eats up plenty of time.

Clifton turns out to be one of the more captivating sites to which SP operates. As the roadbed comes into town it emerges out of a steeply walled riverbed to almost become part of a local highway, so close are ties to pavement.

Out of the train crews' line of sight and hidden by a hill are the tall stacks of a smelter, the reason why the crew is working. Descending from the hill, often literally through backyards of some residences, is the Phelps-

Dodge railroad, striking out for a connection with SP. As the arriving Clifton Branch train pulls into town across a bridge and into a walled-in wide spot defined as a yard, the strong blast of air horns is heard echoing down from on high.

With brakes set hard for a steep descent, a trio of Phelps-Dodge GP38s in Confederate grey livery holds three-dozen cars in restraint. Two units are on the point, the third attached on the rear in a somewhat unusual arrangement, one which P-D finds most suitable for holding back tonnage on a sharply dropping descent.

A ballet of sorts now ensues.

While Southern Pacific's train holds short of the junction, Phelps-Dodge's copper hauler enters a tiny yard crammed between two vertical rock walls. Its train is too lengthy, so the head end pulls on through. Now the rear unit cuts off, running partway back uphill toward the smelter. Meanwhile, 20 or so head-end cars have been split off and shoved down a second track. Then, the two head-end units run around the cars and connect up with the onetime rear-end diesel to form a three-unit lashup.

Hardly has this been done when an SP air horn reverberates between rock parapets. This newcomer takes about half its train length into the yard and then it too retreats light, back from where it came.

Phelps-Dodge power backs down to this half, slowly working it upgrade to a stop, clearing SP roadbed. The seven GP35s repeat their performance once more, then retreat a respectful distance. Now the front portion of what is to become a Phelps-Dodge movement is backed down upon the rear. An air brake test follows, and a grinding run begins as the short but steep climb to the smelter is encountered.

That train has barely disappeared when SP's crew swings into action, red and grey units manhandling two separate cuts into a solitary one with locomotives and caboose at the extremes. A required air brake test is made, and approximately 30 minutes following arrival in Clifton the lead GP35 unit is pointed Lordsburg's way.

There's urgency now, as slightly over six hours have elapsed since a crew went on duty. Just ahead lie several miles of exceptionally slow track, requiring some time before even 30-mph roadbed is reached. A tight squeeze on hours-of-service limits is a real possibility; should it happen, there's no particular problem as a taxi will come out from Lordsburg for the crew, and no other schedule is destined to operate.

Often the power that works into Clifton comes back to Lordsburg to be plugged into a Tucson-bound general freight that works this portion of the Lordsburg Subdivision. Besides traffic coming out of Clifton, it picks up cars from the Globe-Miami Branch, a 133-mile-long extension that has lost a lot of vitality from the closing of copper pits at its extreme. Once a source of long daily trains in either direction, this line now sees perhaps two trains a week at best, leading SP to plea for abandonment. Still, there is enough at Bowie some days to create switching chores for the Lordsburg–Tucson run. Cars for the line are handled off to the side as mainline trains flash by from one end of the division to the other.

Further west at Benson there's a connection with the Douglas Branch, also a source of copper carloadings. As cars are picked up there, the Tucson-bound train extends its length even further. Westbounds originating in Lordsburg frequently contain a mid-train helper as a short hill here and there otherwise proves too difficult to surmount.

Sometime during midsummer, late July through August, another face of the Southwest puts in an appearance. An unlikely bout of rainfall, dubbed locally "the monsoon season," descends abruptly upon landscape and railroad alike. Great cumulous clouds arc high across successive waves of mountaintops, bringing localized downpours that often turn off as abruptly as they begin. Not for nothing do the instructions for the Lordsburg Subdivision list a series of high water detectors for bridges.

Years ago railroaders coined "The Stormy" as a nickname for 165 miles of Tucson Division's corridor from the continually humming terminal at Tucson to Lordsburg. It certainly fits the image in late summer when traffic is normally at its annual peak, with close to 40 trains a day. Weather is often as turbulent on either side of that stretch, towards Yuma or the Texas state line, but somehow the stretch east of Tucson, a lengthy roller coaster of a ride called "Stormy," seems to be inundated with the heaviest downpours.

Fancy now that you have centered your attention upon Tucson, Arizona.

A new day dawns hesitatingly at first, just a faint rim on the eastern horizon as a Kansas City-bound run (KCLAT) out of West Colton's hub just a few hours ago slips out of the yard, beckoned ahead by a brilliant emerald circle. Ahead for the new crew is just under four hours of heavy-duty railroad exertion. Soon the silver trailers and brightly colored containers are rocking despite heavy, continuously welded rail. The altitude at Tucson is a deceptive 2,400 feet, a far cry from the below sea-level readings alongside California's Salton Sea.

Climbing ever since, the desert has been deceiving in its modest rise, only becoming obvious at a point or two like Mohawk Pass which cuts through a narrow band of mountains of the same name on an abbreviated amount of .9% slope from both directions. On a highway little note would be made of such change but an engineer adjusting his set of hefty V-20 engines with throttle changes would be well aware of the nuances.

Coming in from its Los Angeles area genesis the piggybacker paused just long enough for a crew change, a bit of running gear investigation and the addition of one more unit. Commonplace adjustments on heavier schedules see an extra bit of muscle thrown into the consist from Tucson to El Paso in order to maintain the pace over several moderate grades.

144

From time to time this area offers an opportunity to view run-through power off such roads as Rio Grande, Milwaukee Road and Katy. The foreign road power will at times go all the way to Los Angeles, but more usually will be cycled back from Tucson to eastern connections.

Extra units are especially reserved for what are currently termed "expedited trains" with time-sensitive traffic, another name for "hotshot."

Four major hills lie athwart LAKCT's next few hours of existence as it progresses over one of several subdivisions on its several hundred miles' long jaunt from birth to dismemberment. Outside of a possible assist up Beaumont Hill just east of West Colton's giant yard setting the trailers will never again need helpers attached to their consist, since an extra unit at Tucson just creates a larger road engine.

East of Tucson, about 40 miles' worth of essentially double-tracked line pushes over a fissure lying between the Rincon and Empire mountain ranges. At times separated by several hundred yards, twin tracks go from Tucson's 2,400-foot altitude to an approximately 4,000-foot reading at Mescal, where single track takes over. From there it is downgrade through Benson on some 1.0 to 1.3% incline which is just steep enough to require an occasional helper on heavy tonnage westbounds. Not intermodal trains, mind you, but a heavy drag or so each day that caters to copper industry shippers.

The next "topout" comes at Dragoon, 4,500 feet up the ladder 30 miles east of Mescal and site of a 15,000-foot-long siding which provides

For all of its many hundreds of miles of desert look, Tucson Division has only a few areas where cactus is close upon the roadbed. One of the exceptions occurs in Mohawk Pass between Gila Bend and Maricopa.

plenty of room to maneuver trains or plug in more than a single train at a time. There is a need for this kind of flexibility because of bunching, a commonplace event in high-density territory. Two, three hours may go by without a movement past a particular point, then all of a sudden three, four trains zoom by in a short span of time.

Past Dragoon there are two more peaks and valleys before Lordsburg is encountered. The most significant is at Steins with a bit of 1.4% to either flank, slowing both EB and WBs a bit. Then it's across a dry lake bed into Lordsburg and a quick exchange of crews.

On a cloudless day, of which there are still many past the befouled air of cities like Phoenix and Tucson, a good place to be is Mondel siding on the Lordsburg Subdivision. Stein's Pass, a rock-strewn gap through the Peloncillo Mountain chain, lies five miles west up 1.4% ruling grade, while the division point at Lordsburg is 15 miles east over a flat, arrow-straight line drawn upon South Alkali Flat, a dry lake bed. Sometimes heavy squall lines and blowing dust obscure SP, mostly though train action can routinely be eyeballed to both ends because of the change in altitude.

A not untypical observation on a date late in 1986 revealed this tableau.

A late afternoon sun distributed lengthy shadows on the parched landscape as a pure piggyback on a westbound heading was just topping Stein's Pass, thundering by a holed-up EB drag that was waiting for red to turn green momentarily. Meanwhile, Amtrak's thrice-weekly *Sunset Limited* could be seen approaching the fringes of Lordsburg, having just skipped by another EB, a double-stacked set of containers (AXAVT) heading toward New Orleans under contract to American President Lines.

Twenty miles. Four trains in sight!

A minute slice of Tucson Division action, the sort of spectacle generally reserved to the perspective of a dispatcher's control board.

Only on the desert—and there are many such locales—is the three-dimensional model available.

The desert landscape is basically uneven west of Lordsburg, the railroad finding its way from valley to valley through an opening which by comparison with the coastal territory is quite wide. The surface changes in subtle fashion frequently to the accompaniment of multiple ridges that fall away into increasing dark lines on a far horizon. The artful work of some unknown surveyor was responsible for placing curved ribbons where the climb was least.

It is, however, quite modest when compared with the crawling, grasping theme of defeating Tehachapi, or the 7,000-foot heights profiled in the Sierra Nevada, or the walled-in forests that fill much of Oregon.

From Lordsburg into El Paso the line has little to mention except for the final few miles of gentle descent into El Paso. Otherwise it is quite straight and as fast as a speedboard dictates. That means 70 mph for both

146

With the ex-Rock Island trackage now a part of SP the Golden State line north of El Paso has been reborn. Once lonely siding that was rarely occupied, it now moves to the drumbeat of full mainline status. Arabella siding is the locale here, not too far away from the old terminal at Tucumcari, N.M.

Amtraks and authorized freights, those with urgent on their timing. There are a lot of those.

El Paso is a medium-sized terminal, more noted these days for separating traffic into that bound for Kansas City and that destined for San Antonio and beyond now that ex-Rock Island trackage has been incorporated into SP. It also represents a connection with international traffic into Mexico.

Two yards, an older one downtown plus a second known as Chamizal Yard on the eastern side of town, carry the burden locally. San Antonio Division rail skirts eastward toward the Big Bend country of Texas, while the significantly added importance of Carrizozo Subdivision continues Tucson Division activity on for an additional 331 miles to Tucumcari, once the handover terminal between SP and the late Rock Island.

The torrent of train doings that reaches a crescendo between Tucson and El Paso is muted at either end with Phoenix siphoning off some westbound tonnage, reducing ever so slightly what goes to Southern California. Sunset Route and Golden State Route runs go their separate ways east of El Paso. The two trails have remarkably similar first stages; the 309-mile-long Valentine Subdivision to Sanderson, and the 331-mile Carrizozo Subdivision to Tucumcari where the Rock Island once stopped.

Texas is turned over to the San Antonio Division, while Tucumcari is a part of Tucson Division's playing field. The blowing, gritty dust that marks desert railroading continues across extensive tracts of the New Mexico highlands.

This line has always had potential but was seeing less and less traffic until Espee acquired the Rock Island to Kansas City. Gradually the train flow increased, held back initially by the impoverished condition of the Rock's roadbed, but once the rehabilitation project was complete the Golden State Route bloomed at both ends. As activity swelled, crews were sent from El Paso all the way through to Tucumcari, but were dying on the road under the hours-of-service law, in part because the line, although signaled, is not a CTC installation, and sidings are often two-dozen miles apart. Even prior to application of the DTC method of dispatching there were few open train order offices, often cumbersome meets as volume gained.

Twilight falls across the sparsely settled eastern New Mexico plain as an Espee freight does what it has been doing all day and all night since it left Kansas City, gobble up the mileposts.

To illustrate, at one time there was an open office at Vaughn. The next one north was at Tucumcari, 102 miles away. This was fine before El Paso–Kansas City became a mainline railroad once again.

Reverting to a prior arrangement, crews today make two hops, El Paso–Carrizozo and Carrizozo–Tucumcari.

An oddity of the Carrizozo Subdivision is its variety of block signals. The old-style semaphore signal is alive and still controlling drab grey diesels on the New Mexico highlands. Single mounts, double mounts, home and distant signals of the past are interspaced with more modern stock. If you want to view just about any type of block signals that SP has installed since the 1920s, this is where to look. The familiar searchlight model with its single lens, the most recent back-to-back styling with a trio of separate colors. Both appear in large numbers, interspaced with long miles of red and yellow semaphore blades.

Like steel heading straight east from El Paso, the Carrizozo Sub is free-running country, unhampered by any but the barest of built-up areas. Alamogordo with its atomic age reputation is about the largest. Otherwise it is open country, though not necessarily the fastest, for one's impression of the desert must be tempered by the reality of a landscape. Most of El Paso–Tucumcari is a succession of ups and downs, a five-mile pull followed by a 10-mile descent, then more of the same all over again. There are no outstanding geographic features as rails sweep across the highlands, flowing rather easily to take advantage of whatever lower trail exists. Mesas, draws, plateaus are featured, the horizon always rimmed by parched mountains despite the many summer thunderstorms.

Almost lost in this spaciousness, 110 cars and four diesels seem to take forever to conquer the panorama. It is pure illusion served only at a distance, for a close-in look is sound and fury. Coming west out of Vaughn with full tonnage tied to their tail, a group of red and grey ones slips under Santa Fe's swift-flowing roadbed, working hard on a gradual climb that started back near Santa Rosa and carries on for over 50 miles. This is 30 to 40-mile-an-hour running at best, often slower. Sidings can be 20, as much as 34 miles from one another, so half-hour waits or more in the hole go with the territory.

And if running trains from Tucumcari to El Paso isn't always as swift as the 70-mph grandeur of a Cotton Belt, it is a great deal shorter this way from Kansas City, as more than adequate compensation. Which is why Southern Pacific has returned to the Golden State Route in force.

So it is that Tucson Division begins and ends on exactly the same theme, the Great American Desert. Besides spreading its energy across a geographically heated region, it turns out to be the hottest spectacle of railroading on the entire Southern Pacific. Were one to nominate a candidate for the most efficient use of single track in the entire nation, the 500-odd miles from Yuma to El Paso would be among the finalists.

Opposite: The No. 2 track crosses under the No. 1 track near Marsh—east of Tucson.

As an outlying division point sans terminal, Lordsburg is probably the busiest on SP's southern route. Scenes like this with two trains in town simultaneously are a routine happening.

A divided main stem with two separate bridges carries traffic across the El Paso city limits westwards. An early morning pig train heads across one span with Los Angeles its ultimate goal.

RUN, RUN, RUN

Southern Pacific east of El Paso

EAST OF EL PASO, TEXAS, lie genes of the old Texas and New Orleans railroad and the technical independence of the St. Louis, Southwestern Railway, better known by its popularized logo, the Cotton Belt. It is also Southern Pacific of a different dimension, a railroad that opens to an amphitheatre of sweeping plain or wooded farmland, a huge tract of land that encompasses several states, not the least of which is Texas. It is where crafty scheduling, well-run terminals, and moderate-sized locomotive sets do more for staying competitive than all the brute horsepower a mountain dispatcher can dream of.

The bulk of Espee's modern four-axled motive power runs off miles east of El Paso. GP-38s, B30-7s and GP40-2s appear more often on prairie trains than they do out west—which is not to say they are not common-place west of El Paso, because they are, particularly along the Sunset Route into Los Angeles—but the majority of them are employed more often in midwestern or southwestern dominions.

The two would-be suitors, Santa Fe and Southern Pacific, started at opposite ends. Santa Fe was and is fundamentally a plains state railroad that worked its way west, coming upon mountains and evolving a methodology to deal with them. Southern Pacific was and is a western railroad that moved eastward, and in the process, found out how you run trains where there weren't tall, difficult granite barriers. Given its background, SP on the average seems to be a little heavier in horsepower in the midwest than Santa Fe.

A shade under 800 miles separates West Colton's giant yard from El Paso, which is almost halfway to Houston and its massive facility, Englewood Yard. Not only is distance great but so is the physical presence. The "other half" is railroading in a style unrecognized save for a few subdivisions out west. Only the number of opposing trains that must be

Opposite: Just about as far as SP can go in the south. Crossing the Huey Long Bridge into downtown New Orleans.

153

met, crew changes and swiftness of inspections are hindrances for the fast ones. Otherwise they operate under a heading listed as "Column 1, Passenger and Authorized Freight," usually "70 mph." As for regular freights, they move fast too, while a bit more prone for siding time or terminal layover. Of course if a yardmaster ties on too many tons while assigning marginal power, over-the-road performance won't garner any accolades. There are many such instances with heavy southwest tonnage trains; it's called "pulling the yard," a Southern Pacific specialty.

After ticking off a fast-paced 147 miles from Lordsburg, New Mexico, freights come down through mountain-rimmed horizons to cross the Rio Grande River just where El Paso and Juarez, Mexico, meet in expansive habitation across many hills. The importance of El Paso to Southern Pacific is its strategic setting at the confluence of two routes: the Sunset and Golden State. EBs diverge and WBs converge in a never-ending drama of western railroading. A fair percentage of trains passing through, especially those using Sunset Route roadbed towards Houston, New Orleans and East St. Louis will have motive power changed out or altered a bit as they pass through the terminal. Mainly this will happen to the slower movements. As for the important schedules, timetables provide a large measure of alphabet soup symbols that will cruise at passenger train speed, so they'll continue on with their six-axle power or more recently acquired four-motored units without much deletion. That will be their way to the extremes of the system.

El Paso displays its own trains, ones that terminate there from any direction, along with international business generated through Juarez and the Mexican railway system. This will be handled at Cotton Yard, which lies just off the city center, close to the red brick Union Station, a grandiose sounding title from the past that is now livened a bit by the three-times-weekly Amtrak passenger runs in both directions between the Coast and New Orleans. A split between Tucson Division's Carrizozo Sub and San Antonio Division's Valentine Sub occurs at Tower 47 just east of Cotton Avenue, which is exactly where Missouri Pacific (UP) comes aboard, creating a combined SP-MP operation over a 90-mile, single-track district to Sierra Blanca.

If you don't count the old Rock Island line, which is now Cotton Belt's Kansas City Division, a total of four divisions control SP operations east of El Paso to its Mississippi ports, New Orleans, Memphis and East St. Louis. The San Antonio Division, an all-Texas product, runs east to Houston, turns north through Dallas and Ft. Worth and concludes at Denison; Houston Division centers upon huge Englewood Yard, extends southwest into the lower Gulf and northeast to Shreveport, Louisiana. The Lafayette Division is primarily main line out of Houston through Beaumont and on east to New Orleans, with a fair network of branches clustered around the through route. From Shreveport, with a bit of East Texas hill

154

country thrown in, the Cotton Belt completes SP's eastern thrust, carrying traffic across Arkansas to both Memphis and East St. Louis, the road's extremely prominent outlets to eastern and southern rail lines.

Besides Cotton Street, a more expansive facility in El Paso exists at Alfalfa Yard, approximately five miles from downtown and overshadowed by the cracking towers of nearby oil refineries. A flat yard, it serves industrial switching needs, and is also a marshaling yard for interdivisional runs.

Showing what can be done on the modern railroad stage, a single crew takes a train over the 309-mile-long Valentine Subdivision from El Paso to Sanderson, Texas. Yet, in stark contrast, what lies beyond covers only 128 miles, from Sanderson to Del Rio, followed by a 171-mile lap beyond Del Rio to San Antonio's East Yard.

The inconsistency is not in the territory but in the heritage of labor-management bargaining from decades past. For instance, Santa Fe must make a total of 16 crew changes between Los Angeles and Chicago, a heavy burden where intermodal traffic is concerned, as most trains of this nature can routinely whip off the long-standing 100-mile division pay standard in two-plus hours.

Typical suburbia crowns the first few miles of SP east of El Paso; then as the siding sign at Sierra Blanca comes within two dozen miles, there is an initial taste of West Texas. A bit rugged at that. Nothing by comparison with western mountains but a slice of 1% climb to slow matters where desolate, brush-studded land grazes cattle while echoing to the rolling booms of summer's daily thunderstorms. Billowing cumulous clouds in shades that range from brilliant white to dark grey rim the arena as an Espee piggyback tears through Sierra Blanca, leaving MoPac to reach Dallas–Ft. Worth on its own iron.

The seemingly boundless countryside of West Texas spreads ahead, as now only 70-mph track with few restrictions offers its welded surface as a guide. A couple of county seats, a small town in grazing land, rugged looking hills to a clear horizon pass swiftly rearwards, for this is running country.

To railroad this part of America successfully you need space, end to end. Roadbed can gobble up a dozen trains with little impact, given the rapid sequence of remotely controlled sidings that swim by every few miles. In an air-conditioned cab the soft tones of a female voice provide reassurance every five to seven miles as a radio announces "No Defects," an example of technological prowess that hurries. A rash of intermediate ABS signals between sidings are linked to high water detectors, proof positive that frequent though abbreviated storms can cause flash flooding, an undesirable turn of events for high-stepping freight trains.

Centralized traffic control in this area works off microwave instructions with a backup in the track circuits just in case. Microwave instructions come from a computer source which takes into account priority, speed and tonnage in establishing which train takes siding, which holds the main. The track circuitry as a backup system doesn't take complications into account, but merely sets up meets on a first-come, first-served basis, which is vital as support if the main guidance system fails. At each location a small radarlike antenna is pointed towards a distant mountain, usually not more than a dozen miles away. With binoculars, a repeater tower is normally visible.

At the far reaches of their long district, trains slowing down for a crew change at Sanderson get a thorough going over from a green border patrol car. The incoming crew barely leaves the engine when two immigration officers give the locomotive set a detailed search, including every nook and cranny of the prime mover. More than one illegal is usually pulled off a train, often from the oily confines of a 20-cylinder EMD unit.

Sanderson has the look of Southern Pacific past. A sprawling, white wooden depot tops off a small town where mostly old stone buildings display the sun-bleached look of years in cattle country. A rash of cars parked around the station suggest only one thing: a division point, and that it is. Its placement on the Sunset Route suggests impact, a lineup that can run to double figures in 24 hours. Typical of many waypoint spectacles, Sanderson mingles hours of total silence with moments of frenetic haste, a characteristic of the modern railroad, where trains are rarely spaced evenly.

Canyons, draws, arid rolling range country with bouts of flash flooding. That's west Texas, with Sanderson approached from either side by a narrow defile overlooked by red sandstone bluffs. The description fits until Del Rio, where crews are changed once again after crossing one of the railroad's more spectacular bridges across the Pecos River, where a monumental crevasse is both deep and starkly bleak in appearance. The cowboy and cattle likeness of Texas gradually fades east of Del Rio. Rolling hills, trees, and small towns are the scene as SP winds its way east. Hottest thing going on this section of the railroad (as on other subdivisions) is the MBSMFF, a Memphis-originated companion of the long standing Blue Streak Merchandise, these days predominantly a trailer/container/auto rack schedule. Hot off Cotton Belt and east Texas steel, it passes by daily, stops briefly for fresh crewing, then dashes off for El Paso and beyond, covering miles in great gulps. A few hundred miles of open countryside give way to a metropolitan look at San Antonio. Sprawling across several square miles in the modern tradition of western cities, San Antonio is moderately sized in terms of the SP. Part of the cross-country setting, a local traffic base is sandwiched about it. Full trains of rock come in from the west for construction while a local power plant puts SP into the unit coal business, teamed with the omnipresent BN, green in a power pool from northern coal fields.

As single track widens to double on the western edge of town it forms a large "S" in profile, carrying trains past the city center, then angling them on a line towards Houston. Both Missouri Pacific and M-K-T are part of this scene, their activity bringing about several manned interlocking towers, a bit of rarity in this moment of pushbutton control. The upper end of the "S" bends around a weatherbeaten engine terminal, rusting sand towers standing upright to create the familiar SP launching pad complex. Medium sized, it takes care of the local brigade of switch engines plus regional motive power servicing. Lying between it and nearby East Yard is another tower, assigned to control moves through the engine servicing complex and the west end of the yard, since a flat switching lead spills out onto the main.

The dull throbbing of coupled SW-1500s is a constant at this west throat, occasionally overridden, as a brace of four-axled GEs comes in with interchange traffic from the MOP, or a vertically stacked container train is accelerating in a deafening roar onto Flatonia Subdivision rail, the last lap in its trip to Houston's Barbours Cut piers.

The all-Texas San Antonio Division continues its extensive flanks beyond East Yard, reaching across the Flatonia Sub to Glidden where it takes up with Houston Division. Almost to the end is Flatonia Tower, one of the better known regional junctions on this section of the railroad empire. A diamond is formed in the lee of an elderly wooden interlocking plant that continues to function amidst the trendy face of electronics on all sides. About two years ago an errant freight derailed, taking out a goodly portion of the connecting pipe and most everyone figured that meant the end. In an unexpected move, SP repaired the damage in kind, the tower still hooping up orders in 1986, since CTC control from the west fuses into a DTC system on the east.

Flatonia is typical SP; hours of nothing, moments of concentrated bedlam. Houston–San Antonio trains stay to an east-west thrust aboard Flatonia Sub all the way, running off it at Glidden. The line is CTC'd from East Yard to Flatonia where it becomes a Direct Traffic Control system of blocks. The tower exists because of a north-south line, in reality more of a divergence for the bond with San Antonio and beyond. To the north lies the Dalsa line to Hearne and the Ennis Sub, SP's long-enduring transcontinental routing being the significant itinerary, as trains make their way to Cotton Belt territory along with its upriver terminals on the Mississippi. The connection here also explains why ''via Kansas City'' is so desirable on the ''next morning'' train sheet delivered across executive desks in San Francisco. For cards dealing the West Coast–East St. Louis trade, the circuitous Cotton Belt–Flatonia–El Paso haul was always equivalent to a thoroughbred's weight penalty. SP took great pride in its ability to

A westbound piggybacker is about to hit the diamond at Flatonia, Texas. In 1984 a derailed car tore out a goodly portion of this mechanical interlocking tower and to everyone's surprise it was rebuilt with original style piping instead of electronic switches.

schedule the BSM freights across country in record time, but it always had the extra loop through Flatonia and west Texas to contend with, not to mention a need for extra fuel. The rerouting of East St. Louis traffic via Kansas City has diminished Flatonia Tower sightings slightly; however, Memphis Gateway trains still cant to the curve north, bright aluminum trailers reflecting off a ''Tower #3'' in a late afternoon sun.

While Cotton Belt trade comes from a north link at Flatonia, the south exit opens to the lower Gulf Coast, Victoria, Brownsville, the Texas-Mexican RR. A long yard track complements a 10,000-foot siding west of the well-kept tower, an exchange opportunity for the four compass points displayed by Flatonia Tower. Trains originating in Houston and bound for Victoria often come east to Flatonia first rather than go directly southwest from Englewood Yard. Pulling across the diamond west of the tower they frequently pick up cars dropped by locals, then having consolidated their somethings 100 car lengths proceed to back through the interlocking plant to the Dalsa Line prior to heading south to Yoakum and Victoria in an uncommon performance.

East to Houston, north to Hearne, south to coastal waters—this is Southern Pacific running country. Track slips through intermittent fields and low stands of trees at a smooth pace, long gentle curves tied to ex-

A hotshot train out of Los Angeles departs Hearne, Texas, after making a crew change. Ten minutes before it arrived all movement ceased in the small central Texas yard and will only pick up the pace once again when the caboose has cleared the lead.

tended stretches of tangency, mostly with controlled sidings determining who goes, who stops. Ordinary trains flow through this frictionless portion of the SP domain, thoroughbreds fly. Were it not for yards, for blocking needs, no trucker could keep pace.

In Houston, Englewood Yard northeast of downtown's skyscraper embellished profile is to the system's east end what West Colton, Roseville and Eugene represent in a western way. Momentarily, recent upgrades and expansions of capacity are not fully appreciated as the oil patch descends almost as rapidly as it boomed a few years ago. Ever stirring, Englewood won't be handling quite the number of cars this year or next that it expected to, still it's the biggest terminal scene beyond West Colton. Let's guess that instead of observing 35 departures in 24 hours there will only be 28. The drift is that although SP's most prominent eastern yard is doing less these days the lively, animated spirit of a vast terminal operation continues.

Dating in modern form to 1956, Englewood Yard is today on a par with West Colton in terms of the latest that electronics has to sell a railroad. Just recently each one of the 64 bowl tracks was tied into an advanced computer system—is there any other kind?—at the gravity yard's crest. In addition to the main retarders, each bowl track now has a tangent point retarder. Coupled to a radar device, the retarder is fed data on a freight car's weight and speed, then acts accordingly. Taking into account these variables as well as how many other cars are already in a track, the tangent point installation slows each car to a desired coupling speed of four mph.

Prior to the most recent decline in petroleum fortunes—certainly a matter of significance to SP—Englewood Yard was handling between 5,000 and 6,000 cars a day, classifying close to 3,000 of them, while servicing close to 60 trains in the same time frame. About 1,000 industries in and around Houston are serviced from this one huge yard, which in addition to its mighty regional statistics, caters to Sunset Route through needs.

The wide-reaching industrial/petrochemical world that extends 50 miles east of Houston and into western Louisiana needs more than a single terminal, so 25 miles southeast of Englewood on the Galveston Subdivision there are two major installations which perfectly reflect what the area means to Southern Pacific. Strang Yard is termed an industrial support yard. It has 13 classification tracks and a large menagerie of small power, Geeps and SW-1500s, which serve the greatest concentration of petrochemical activity in the world. A seven-day-a-week place, it handles up to 700 cars a day, perhaps 8-10 schedules, with trains going to the far reaches of SP—East St. Louis, Los Angeles and New Orleans. Geared to nearby petrochemical plants, most outbound traffic is worked at night; inbound cars are primarily a daylight job. Blocking several trains at Strang relieves Englewood Yard of the chore.

The best known outbound is the SRCRK-SRASK chemical train,

which originates in Strang, then runs to Pine Bluff six days a week where it splits. The SRCRK is a run-through schedule handed over to Conrail at East St. Louis to be forwarded to Enola, Pennsylvania, while the other portion is transferred to the Alton and Southern RR.

Down the road from Strang is Barbours Cut intermodal terminal, primarily built for mini-bridge or land-bridge container business. Built in 1979, it consists of two working tracks that hold 58 cars and two storage tracks with a 52-car capacity. The international trade is responsible for the double-stacked container trains you see highballing across the southwest to both Barbours Cut and New Orleans. The 55-mile-long Galveston Subdivision, anchored upon Englewood, is responsible for a little more than 50% of the railroad's southwestern petrochemical carloadings.

Like any of Espee's major terminals, Englewood Yard is central to

A double set of SW-1500s goes over the gravity hump at Englewood Yard in the summer of 1985. Typical of many trains' makeup is the set of cars waiting to be classified.

161

Houston Division action. From it flow the locals, the industrial switchers and the through Sunset Route trains from San Antonio and New Orleans. Add in the through traffic to other parts of SP, plus regional dispatching, and scope of this yard is perceived.

Off to the southwest lies the flatland railroading associated with Gulf Coast destinations, a fair portion of which is run over Missouri Pacific trackage rights. While SP has segments of its own, down in the far corner of the state at Brownsville, the bulk of mileposts to reach it are framed in a MoPac lettering style. The area here represents an outlet into the Mexican railway system via MoPac interchange. At Alice, the Texas-Mexican Railway is used to connect SP with the NdeM at Laredo. Due to its lengthy border straddling from the Pacific Ocean to Gulf waters, SP offers more ports of entry to Mexico than any other U.S. railroad. Compared with other destinations out of Englewood, the number of trains sent into lower Gulf yards isn't heavy, but the lines there provide their share of system revenue.

Besides Sunset Route importance, two other major routings out of Englewood are significant. A plot of Houston shows SP as a rough circular

The petrochemical industry which is so much a part of the southwest region of SP is clearly in evidence at Galveston, Texas, where a couple of Geeps and a local are waiting while the crew takes time out for a meal.

162

form with Englewood Yard off on a north, northeast tack (in seafarers' parlance). Between downtown and the busy yard lies Hardy Street, the busy engine terminal and shops, far enough away so that power moves between the yard and engine servicing tracks are made by hostlers, frequently with eight or 10 units at a time.

A complex railroad city, Houston abounds with junctions, towers and crossings, much of them under control of the Houston Belt and Terminal Railroad, whose bright yellow switchers are seen everywhere. HB&T rails run right underneath the hump lead to Englewood Yard; the same rails are crossed at grade on departure tracks to the east at Tower 87, these days a remote-controlled bank of relays.

Thrusting off a bit northwest from Englewood is a line to Dallas–Ft. Worth, which carries, in addition to the normal types of trains one sees between Texas's two largest cities, the pioneering Sprint trains, the road's entrance into high-frequency, short trailer trains. The emphasis in Sprint is on frequency, over a 264-mile high-speed course that encompasses two subdivisions, the Hearne Sub north out of Houston, and the Ennis Subdivision from Hearne to Miller Yard on the south end of Dallas. Sprint is a cabooseless run with a reduced crew, usually of a very short consist to ensure expedited handling. It is assigned a single unit of the latest classes, either a 4800-series GP38-2 or a GP40-2.

Since its introduction to the Dallas–Houston corridor, Sprint has been added to other train sheets. Service now goes north from Dallas to St. Louis. On the West Coast, Portland–Klamath Falls and Los Angeles–Phoenix have been added to the list of Sprint pairings. Next step, possibly Los Angeles–Bay Area?

A binding relationship between SP territory and the Cotton Belt is forged from Englewood Yard to Shreveport. The chemical trains that originate from Strang head this way, as does all the Texas-north action that rolls on the St. Louis-Southwestern. Relatively little of this particular line is block signaled, so the application of DTC and radio speeds up train handling in territory which has grown in stature.

"K" trains are a common breed on all the lines out of Englewood. In SP terms, a "K" is any train handling cars placarded with such hazardous materials as "Explosives A," "Poison Gas," "Radioactive" or any of a baker's dozen of tongue-twisting chemical compounds that the petrochemical world produces. Given the company that SP keeps around Houston the symbol "K" is affixed to many train lists behind the "Extra ———." They require a rolling inspection by the outbound crew at all crew-change locations.

Combined in an operating timetable with Houston Division, the Lafayette Division is a little-advertised part of the railroad. Although it is overwhelmed by the publicity accorded transcontinental business between West Coast and midwest terminals, the Lafayette Division is certainly no backwater operation. Generically, it too is a railroad of petrochemicals, plastics and intermodal schedules, the latter growing in significance with land-bridge development. As previously listed, almost 60% of southwest petrochemical waybills come spilling out of the Galveston Sub where Strang Yard lies. Much of the rest is contributed by two nearby Lafayette Division parts, the Sabine Branch—Beaumont to Port Arthur—and a strung-out complex astride mainline territory around Lake Charles, Louisiana. After wandering through the Houston–Port Arthur–Lake Charles network of SP roadbed, one gets an impression that every tank car in existence is either there or will soon be, so extensive is oil and its derivatives.

The basic thrust of Lafayette Division is a continuation of the Sunset Route to its eastern extremity at New Orleans. Revolving around this fundamental east-west axis are several branches in Louisiana plus a couple in eastern Texas which play a key role in tonnage statistics because of their proximity to the oil industry. The Sabine Branch runs down to water's edge, to an inlet from the Gulf of Mexico where several large refineries are spread over a cluttered shoreline. Many other oil-related industries line the tracks between Port Arthur and Beaumont. Using nearby Beaumont Yard on the main stem as a base, trains slip north over the non-signaled Rockland Branch to Lufkin, where they make connection with Houston Division for a run to Shreveport and the Cotton Belt. It represents not only a shortcut north, but keeps that much traffic off Englewood Yard's ever busy retarders. Loads from Shreveport will go to Pine Bluff's gravity yard for classification into the chemical/oil trains that spring from the Galveston Sub.

In concert with the unsurpassed physical surroundings along SP, the line across southern Louisiana has few peers in appearance. Water level to the extreme, it features swampy marshland, countless bridges and seemingly endless flirtations with waterways, natural and artificial. In fact, one of the division's greatest crosses is a drawbridge astride the intracoastal waterway at Morgan City, Louisiana. Treated to a new heavy-duty lift span in 1971, the bridgework was hit by errant barges 57 times in its first 22 months of existence. Regular accidents, typically minor, are a common occurrence where the intracoastal waterway is spanned.

Hinged to Englewood Yard on its west, the Lafayette Division covers 352 miles through the bayous and parishes of Louisiana to Avondale Yard just short of New Orleans. Some trains are broken up there, becoming interchange blocks to different railroads; others pause for a transfer crew to guide them across the Mississippi River on the celebrated Huey Long Bridge, becoming run-throughs on Norfolk Southern and CSX.

Beaumont Yard, Lake Charles Yard and Lafayette Yard in a west-to-east rank, are the more significant intermediate terminals on this division. Until recently, oil rig and shipbuilding were booming, and the line is dotted

Just before Amtrak took over, the daily *Sunset Limited* to New Orleans was passing across one of the many watering holes in Louisiana as a trio of "fishermen" marked its passage.

with small to large marine firms besides chemical plants. A fair menu would be four to six through trains daily in each direction, plus a fair contingent of locals—more on the western half than elsewhere.

Track is good for 55 mph, a bit less than on other division mains across the southwest, while Centralized Traffic Control is not in evidence. So much traffic turns north out of Texas that the line east of Houston is considered a shade less significant—though not by much.

Since cross-country, interdivisional runs are SP, the dramatic difference in profile along the southwest sunbelt, say between that of Tucson Division and Lafayette Division should come as no surprise. For over 200 miles west of New Orleans a line profile shows the barest of rise, essentially depicted as a straight line. The greatest upgrade is shown as 1/10th of 1%, hardly qualifying as much. Although this essentially water level route is so flat, it is unusual to find so many six-motored units latched on the point. The four-axled units so common north and east of Englewood Yard are not all that routine on the road to New Orleans. This is because so much activity in Louisiana is geared to West Coast connections, such as AVLAT (Avondale-Los Angeles Trailers) or a BAAVT (Bay Area-Avondale Trailers).

From bridge to bridge, alongside miles of watery marsh, the SP east of Houston is no different railroad. Only the landscape changes, the end result of erecting hundreds of different mileposts.

Sprint trains aside, SP's north Texas performance has shrunk a bit

165

recently. Two reasons exist, one internal, one external. The outside factor comes from the MoPac-UP merger, reducing interchange formerly handed over to the SP, particularly around Ft. Worth, where Cotton Belt has sharply curtailed its presence as a result. The internal cause revolves around the ex-Rock Island line, since many trains now head due west from East St. Louis rather than down through Pine Bluff. Transcontinental routing was and is through East Texas, bypassing Houston, so any effects on tonnage would be felt there. Where SP put its capital improvement money to give it a well-publicized "all CTC or double-track line" between West Coast and midwest points was to the north of Flatonia. Routing is Hearne on the Ennis Sub, thence to Corsicana on Cotton Belt rail then across Texas to Tyler, Mt. Pleasant, Texarkana and Pine Bluff. It is a land-scape of easy running and long sidings, a race track followed by high steppers of a diminished breed now that Kansas City points west too.

From Hearne to Corsicana, 90 fast-paced miles, Sprint trains mingle with the long, heavy transcontinentals, creating a dramatic imprint of what SP can do. No passenger trains exist to establish a sense of priority; yet the expedited freights equal their caliber.

The animated lifestyle of Hearne seems to go on hold several minutes prior to the arrival of an LAMFF (Los Angeles-Memphis Fast Freight) with its well-heeled 4.0-hp per ton motive power ratio, twice that of common freights. A double set of switchers, heretofore engaged in flat switching long cuts of big hopper cars, halts. A made-up freight headed north to Dallas patiently idles, two B30-7s held in check. At a nearby MoPac grade crossing a red block shines bright, holding one of that road's trains in its commanding embrace.

All is in readiness for the expected entrance, just as in days past, a first-class ranking in the timetable rated similar attention.

Hundreds of miles successfully completed, the LAMFF has many more to face before slipping across the Mississippi River into Memphis. Charging into Hearne, bleeding off speed by the simple expedient of drifting, five 3,000-hp-plus units clatter noisily to a stop. Looking a bit weatherbeaten from their long years in tunnels and mountain passes out west they will be off and running momentarily. New faces in the cab, two short blasts played on an air horn freshly goaded, the group of veteran, high-mileage diesels gather momentum. Across the MoPac diamond they accelerate, the final cars clearing yard limits in a cadence of steel upon steel, bursting forth like a machine gun. Given all that power, what else could happen?

Hearne can breathe normally now.

North of Corsicana, beyond the junction with Cotton Belt, Ennis Subdivision carries business on to Dallas and beyond, concluding up near the Oklahoma border at Denison. South of Dallas at Garret, a track heads off with a Ft. Worth connection where it ties into the SSW coming west from the direction of Mt. Pleasant, a line that probably carries, at most, four through trains daily. The local CB yard in Ft. Worth has been all but shuttered recently, its functions transferred over to Miller Yard in Dallas. Besides handling Sprint trains, Miller dispatches trains north and south, to Houston via Hearne, north to Denison or east to the Cotton Belt through a link at Plano on the north end.

Location. Direction. Imprecise terms at best. If you live on the East Coast, St. Louis Southwestern develops that western look. To people who establish schedules or monitor trains for Southern Pacific, the Cotton Belt represents the system's eastern establishment. No matter the relative bearings or the role of Arkansas's big hump yard, hundreds of miles of top speed roadbed place the Pine Bluff Division on an equal footing with anywhere else that SP operates.

Cotton Belt country! What better sampling technique exists than a discussion of Pine Bluff Yard, which until the Rock Island trackage was hoisted aboard, was the sole kingpin of its multi-state spread.

The Pine Bluff Division encompasses all of the original St. Louis Southwestern Railway, from East St. Louis to Ft. Worth and Corsicana, Texas, *et al.,* an extended, slim railroad of superior grooming that is principally main line in character. The division revolves around the performance of a gravity yard in central Arkansas. On a comparative basis, it is little more than half the size of Houston's Englewood Yard, but is situated in a quite different context. There aren't hundreds of industries, a petroleum industry or extensive port facilities to keep Pine Bluff charged up, spawning dozens of locals. The pressure of Pine Bluff arises from a strategic position in the system, a need to split up, block and rearrange through trains east or west. Descriptively, it is the nerve center of a bridge-type railroad.

Forty-two classification tracks and a flat switching yard routinely classify 2,000–2,500 cars into any of 70 separate blocks daily. Every train out of Pine Bluff has at least one, and some have as many as nine blocks. On an average day, somewhere around 50 trains arrive and leave daily, keeping in mind that inbound trains after being carved up become out-bound trains as well. Carloadings arriving from Memphis, or from East St. Louis, often do so on run-through moves from other railroads needing to be placed in orderly rank for movement west. Neither of those locations does any blocking on their own. That is left to Pine Bluff.

Before Cotton Belt added the Kansas City Division to its physique, daily train sheets on the Pine Bluff Division recorded more action. Now East St. Louis dispatches many brawny diesels through stands of MoPac signals to Kansas City and on down to Tucumcari, rather than downriver to Illmo and Pine Bluff, bypassing the gravity yard's crest while shortening cross-country running time. Notable among trains now absent from Pine Bluff is the Blue Streak Merchandise, though its companion hotshot, the

Memphis Blue Streak Merchandise, still passes through on its flying trip west.

Adding to its stature is Pine Bluff's position as the chief maintenance depot for newer GE power, the large group of four-axled B30-7s that primarily roam lines east of El Paso. During the '60s and '70s the big 8600-series U-boats were assigned here, the locals claiming they kept them in better running condition than coast shops did in later years. The bulk of Espee's diesel roster is of course EMD, with Houston, Roseville and Eugene Shops serving up mainly running repairs, Los Angeles offering heavy-duty maintenance, while Sacramento General Shops rebuilds from the frame up.

The Cotton Belt explains itself as a bridge carrier with slightly more than 60% of its total traffic coming from other railroads, including SP lines. That is a view from within, for SP officialdom hardly sees its place as anything but an operating division, one of nine that comprise the total system. This separatist attitude is quite prevalent on Cotton Belt no matter who actually calls the shots, a sort of regional *esprit de corps.*

End to end a mainline railroad, as its paucity of branch lines suggests, Cotton Belt nonetheless spawns a good number of locals during summer to early fall, handling a regional harvest season especially on the Jonesboro Subdivision north of Pine Bluff. With its role as a bridge route confirmed, the road adds in solid trainloads of rice and soybeans, carried in flat grey hopper cars with CB lettering that seem to be everywhere west on SP. The biggest single source of such traffic is at Stuttgart where a single shipper may provide up to 300 carloads a week in late September and early October. Hauled south to Pine Bluff Yard, the hoppers are sorted out through the firm grip of clattering retarders for all parts of the nation.

Beyond Pine Bluff north or south, the greatest impression of Cotton Belt railroading would be the hustling, momentary passage of high-speed freight trains. Working south from the East St. Louis area, Cotton Belt trains ride across Missouri Pacific rail, cruising downriver alongside the Mississippi, crossing it to Illmo and entering home territory. Now come opportunities for speed that will match anyone's. Over the majority of the 657 miles that carry a train from Illmo to the SP connection at Corsicana, Texas, the hogger's bible, "Maximum Authorized Speed for Trains," states in bold face, under the heading "All Trains": "70 mph." Only the Tyler Sub in east Texas calls for something less, and that is a slightly reduced 65-mph maximum. Two mainline connecting links, the 68-mile-long Memphis Subdivision, which is ex-Rock Island track, holds to a maximum 50-mph standard, while the lines out of Lewisville into Shreveport, and from Mt. Pleasant into Ft. Worth are topped out at 49 mph, being primarily non-signaled territory.

Although it has no automatic block signals, the Shreveport Sub-division, which heads south from a connection at Lewisville, is important,

Pine Bluff, Arkansas, saw early-on runthrough power. The Penn Central in the late '60s linked up on a train that came through the East St. Louis Gateway direct to the Cotton Belt, and power stayed on to Pine Bluff. The railroad hadn't yet gotten around to masking out the old Pennsy logo at this time.

as it represents a path for Englewood Yard and all the Gulf Coast points. Three to four freight trains each way daily are average.

The SP, or, if you prefer, Cotton Belt's easternmost penetration across the river from St. Louis offers rather modest terminal facilities. It primarily serves as a gatekeeper, with only a modest amount of marshaling action. Blocking will be taken care of at Pine Bluff or, to a lesser degree, at Kansas City.

The East St. Louis yard is pinched between ICG to the south and a large Alton and Southern terminal on the north. Quite a few trains carry the initials "AS" in their symbol, a clue to how much the terminal road trades with Espee. The engine facilities are jammed into a corner where Terminal RR Assoc. of St. Louis maintains an interlocking plant, so that on a round-the-clock basis, long interchange cuts mingle with long trains, often imposing terminal delay on the Cotton Belt. East St. Louis has inherited a role of moving trains, not taking a lengthy view of them. A fair part of the work involves run-through trains, especially with Conrail and the Norfolk Southern. While red and grey power is frequently seen to the east because of these run-throughs, Pine Bluff engine terminal services and turns quite a bit of power off the two roads mentioned.

Not all terminal delay is caused by outside sources. Given its quite modest size, and its narrow cross-section, East St. Louis creates some of its own. A rather common scene south of TRRA's interlocking, and on

MoPac steel, is a couple of StLSWs strung out waiting for an outbound to leave so they can tie up. Inactive, the faded lashups of big C-Cs out of the west are cast in a totally unaccustomed character. Other than unit coal trains on other carriers, the brawniest sets of motive power striding the local roadbed on both sides of the Mississippi come from SP or its subsidiary.

Once totally committed to the southbound moves through Pine Bluff, East St. Louis now divides its interest between Kansas City and the Arkansas yard. The spectacle of big tunnel motors crawling across the Misssisipi River behind a Terminal RR cut is no longer unusual.

Rail to rail, four feet eight and one-half inches. Take your pick, East St. Louis, Pine Bluff, Hearne, Lafayette and a hundred other towns. Exactly the same width out west, too. The difference lies in the surroundings, in the pace, in the look of Southern Pacific's east end.

Drizzling rain collects in rivulets on a red nose leading 5,500 tons west through the piney woods of southern Arkansas, prime movers at full voice reacting to an always appearing row of green lenses. Way south in Gulf Coast country, a complete train's worth of double-stacked container cars is pulling across the Mississippi River on Huey Long's namesake bridge, and at the very same moment, a piercing siren floats over the crest of Englewood Yard as a lengthy cut of petrochemical cars approaches waiting retarders. On the fringe of the great bend country of Texas an MBSMFF casts its looping headlight from side to side, a twinkling atom of brightness in a sea of darkness.

The other half of the zebra's stripes.

Opposite: Just in from Houston, a trainload of double-stacked containers moves out of Avondale Yard toward Huey Long Bridge and on to nearby New Orleans for transfer to a waiting ship.

The land bridge intermittently takes to water along the Gulf Coast. Almost at the end of its journey that began on the West Coast an eastbound train of stacked containers crosses a coastal inlet close to New Orleans.

171

A hostler brings a set of units in from Englewood Yard for servicing while the Houston skyline reaches upward in the background. Unlike other major SP yards the diesel facilities at Houston are located at a separate though nearby point.

A rainy day envelops Stuttgart, Arkansas, on the Cotton Belt where a Geep is busily engaged in shuffling covered hoppers to nearby rice storage plants. This area provides hundreds of car-loadings to the railroad each year.

An entire trainload of sand and gravel for local building projects is dragged through downtown San Antonio behind a couple of GP-40s.

As in most of the southwest, SP's track through west Texas is characterized by numerous creeks which are dry 98% of the time. It's the other 2% of raging, torrential rainfall that gives the railroad trouble.

THE ROCK IN RED AND GREY

The Golden State Route belongs to SP

A S THE BANKRUPT ROCK ISLAND exited American railroading's roll of charter members, Southern Pacific most appropriately cast its herald eastward to Kansas City, restoring the same steel that had been formally abandoned just hours before. Over many decades the California-based carrier had parlayed an on-again, off-again relationship with the Chicago, Rock Island and Pacific into one of its major eastern connections, known as the ''Golden State Route.'' The route's career had proved to be checkered, surging to real importance in some decades, dwindling to the status of a poor cousin in others, especially the past 10 years or so, when its decline didn't help RI's ability to survive.

When Southern Pacific initially took over responsibility for operating the Kansas City–to–Tucumcari section of the just-expired Rock Island, things were probably as bad as they could be to still qualify as an ''operating railroad.'' One can only imagine the consternation that reigned when Espee officials made their initial visit to a route they desired for its geographic connections, discovering its true shape. As an example, when the first SP crews were dispatched west out of Herington, Kansas, they were ''dying on the road'' by application of the hours-of-service rule only 60 miles from their terminal, not because of heavy opposing traffic on this single-track railroad but because maximum allowable velocity was 10 mph, hardly enough to guard against derailment on such unkempt routing.

To which must be added delays associated with perhaps meeting an opposing move, although there certainly weren't many of these until SP had a chance to rebuild.

It was, in blunt terms, a disastrous piece of track, all 600-odd miles of it. Regardless, from Southern Pacific's standpoint it represented an opportunity. There would be access to new traffic sources, and connections through the important Kansas City gateway. Competitive standards could also be maintained in light of the Union Pacific-Missouri Pacific combo

Opposite: The flat openness of southwestern Kansas is clearly evident as an eastbound LACHT (Los Angeles–Chicago TOFC/COFC) train speeds by a train in the hole.

175

just being forged, and there was a great opportunity to shave miles, plenty of them, off the existing Cotton Belt routing to the West Coast, which up to now had to circle way south into Texas by way of San Antonio.

Check for instance Espee's historical routing for the BSMFF. The pacesetter among the railroad's transcontinental schedules, it competed with Santa Fe and Union Pacific rivals for carloadings, but always at a disadvantage, for the extended loop that wanders through San Antonio and the Big Bend country of Texas adds several dozen more miles to SP trains, compared to the opposition. An additional handicap was that the SP does not have long stretches of double track to smooth operations as do the others.

Miles are time, a feature not particularly bothersome in prior eras but of critical importance now. The trailers—forwarder traffic plus autos and auto parts—are today's most vital traffic, and he who runs fastest retains an advantage. This is where ex-Rock iron fits into the scheme, providing a shortcut out of East St. Louis, as compared to the original itinerary through Pine Bluff, Arkansas.

From its inception as a new SP domain, the onetime Golden State route offered advantages in cross-country moves, notwithstanding its 10-mph limit, given its shorter distance, when combined with trackage rights across Missouri into Cotton Belt yard tracks at East St. Louis.

Initially, not many trains were scheduled, because so much rehabilitation work was under way. Southern Pacific spent millions upgrading the deteriorated Kansas roadbed, in the process creating a new operating division while assigning control to its Cotton Belt subsidiary. Today the Cotton Belt manages it as the Kansas City Division, controlling a significant portion of the railroad's vast empire for through movements, as well as being a source of important local tonnage. This, after all, is America's wheat belt. Roadbed which once bent (quite literally) under the weight of Rock Island motive power is dotted every few miles with grain elevators, producing carloadings for Espee.

Compared to what Southern Pacific contends with on its western lines, the Cotton Belt's Kansas City Division is quite straightforward, a lengthy main stem with hardly any branch-line activity worth mentioning. Main action is concentrated west of Kansas City; some trains east of that important rail terminal are shared as connections with other carriers, while the link to East St. Louis is run entirely over other railroad's steel, principally Missouri Pacific's Northern Division. There is also some use of terminal railroad iron in St. Louis, plus Kansas City.

The Cotton Belt division map shows that its own track extends from Kansas City to East St. Louis, but realistically little money was put into this section of the ex-Rock Island. Labeled Subdivision 1, the 295 miles across Missouri are asterisked by a notation in small print that states the track is out of service between MP 93 and MP 288.3. A small portion of

Opposite: Where once the Rock Island strode, a westbound Cotton Belt train slowly exits Armourdale Yard on its way toward Tucumcari, New Mexico, and beyond.

176

It doesn't happen often but every once in a while the combination of two roads' diesels makes the right profile. Both trains, MoPac and Espee eastbounds, come off the bridge that links Kansas City, Kansas, with Kansas City, Missouri.

the onetime RI is retained at either end for local traffic sources; otherwise Kansas City to East St. Louis is on someone else's rails.

Another glimpse of what Subdivision 1's role is all about can be gleaned by another rule, "six-axle locomotives prohibited on Subdivision 1." On SP, that is tantamount to nothing.

Imagine now that it is a June day in 1986. Pure red and grey imagery dominates the Kansas Division, except for borrowed and run-through power from the likes of Rio Grande, Union Pacific, Burlington Northern and, yes, even Santa Fe. You are in Tucumcari, once a fairly active terminal when Rock Island's first-generation F's represented what was "modern," along with blunt-nosed Alcos out of New York state erecting shops. The locomotives came in from Kansas City or Chicago several times a day, were switched out, their trains handed over to the early vintage black and silver units that would be hustled west to Arizona and California. There would be solid trains of PFE reefers going home for reloads, strings of boxcars, flats and hoppers moving both ways, and clusters of trainmen around the depot, chatting as they swapped runs. Then the long decline set in. The Golden State streamliners were pulled off and a gradual contraction in interchange between the two railroads set in.

Not too long ago Tucumcari as a railroad stop was in sorry physical shape, reflecting the status that had befallen Rock Island. Furthermore, SP had reduced the interchange traffic there so it could hold onto what it generated as long as possible on the east-west haul.

At one time, the Rock had been blessed with a trial run of a solid auto parts train out of Chicago, its destination an assembly plant in California. Before the train made it to Tucumcari an oft-repeated comment among SP officials at the time was that if the RI happened to derail that train, the railroad would be bankrupt. It didn't happen, but little did people realize how poverty stricken Rock Island really was and how soon it would actually succumb.

Now that the line is rejuvenated, the mixed cadence of six-axled motors out of La Grange and slow idling B30-7s is sensed several times a day. Tucumcari's old Spanish-style depot is certainly busier now that SP goes all the way to Kansas City. Seventy-mile-per-hour maximums are now permissible on certain trains and two of Southern Pacific's hottest schedules, the Blue Streak Merchandise Fast Freight (BSMFF) and the CHLAF (Chicago-Los Angeles Forwarders) have been directed to blister rail joints on this extension of the system. The former is an all SP venture, connecting East St. Louis with Southern California, while the latter illustrates just what Kansas City has done for the railroad. In a partnership arrangement, the Burlington Northern brings it into Armourdale Yard out of the windy city in a contest with UP and Santa Fe for a railroad's lifeblood.

The town of Tucumcari, essentially an overnight motel and fast food community on Interstate 40, won't return to the status it had when both RI and SP considered it an end point during dieseldom's first generation. Run-through wasn't known then except on the daily pair of Los Angeles–Chicago streamliners. Freight strictly adhered to home turf and units were pulled off and sent to service tracks for inspection and a return assignment from whence they came. Now the classic depot which once catered to passengers and overalled trainmen is just another Espee crew-change place, worth a few moments' delay on a train sheet while Tucson Division and Kansas City Division crews exchange data about their charges before turning them over.

Most everywhere else, Southern Pacific's mainline action falls under the gaze of CTC machines. Not totally universal, but almost so, because for a single-tracked railroad such methodology allows SP to wring the maximum ability out of its far-flung lines. The Kansas City Division is notable for its lack of CTC initials in a timetable covering seven subdivisions. Along Subdivision 1 the idea is mere rhetoric, as this is really a railroad that isn't, given its near-total shutdown. Subdivision 2 at 296 miles long is run almost 99% on MoPac rails and does contain some CTC control, but only by MP dispatchers. At either end—Terminal Railroad Association in St. Louis and Kansas City Terminal Railroad on the west end—SP trains use these switching roads' territory to reach terminals. Armourdale Yard in Kansas City is much busier now than it was during the final agonies of Rock Island.

Armourdale butts against and parallels the south fringes of UP's larger Armstrong Yard in Kansas City, which turns out to be a convenience, for in working west of this prairie city the Cotton Belt has trackage rights via UP to Topeka. Beyond that point it is home rails over the onetime Rock Island all the way to Tucumcari. As a condition of the Union Pacific-Missouri Pacific merger, SP obtained trackage rights over the two roads, and didn't need to rebuild paralleling portions of a deteriorated roadbed. This preserved a competitive routing between West Coast points and two of midwestern America's most significant rail terminals.

Railroaders outside that merger seem to have a less than sanguine view of the combination, for they tend to refer to its impact upon their own systems as the "MOP-UP."

Nevertheless, acquisition of Rock Island's cross-state track in Kansas seems to have been favorable to SP train movements. During one mid-June Saturday in 1986 seven trains either originated or passed through Armour-dale Yard during a 10-hour daytime segment. Some traffic came from a rerouting of former Pine Bluff Division movements this way; other traffic originated from the connections SP had made by entering into the Kansas City scene.

Southern Pacific through-train symbols are typically an acronym combining the source, the ending destination, and a letter for the predominant type of traffic carried in each train. BAKCT denotes Bay Area (Calif.)-Kansas City Trailers while CHLAF indicates Chicago-Los Angeles Forwarders. This is coupled with a number indicating the date a train originated from its initial terminal. Simply because a train is a T or F doesn't

A cold, wet afternoon descends upon Herington, Kansas, as a crew change is made on a local freight which has dropped its train off a mile back and run forward to the old yard office for the change.

180

designate purity, because boxcars, hoppers, or whatever, often creep into the consist of such moves, and the symbols illustrate the basic consist only. Jack-of-all-trade trains, usually without any overriding priority, have a "Y" affixed to their tail, such as EULAY (Eugene-Los Angeles).

□

Returning to that June day in Armourdale we discover that Cotton Belt's terminal superintendent was frequently in contact with the Chicago and Northwestern, the Burlington Northern, the Milwaukee Road, and the Norfolk and Western about interchange of trains in both directions. He was also being kept current on system traffic carded between East St. Louis and Tucumcari. CNW interchange coming south originated on that road's DWKMA out of Duluth for coupling into SSW's hot running CHLAF, whose origins in Chicago were brought into Armourdale by the BN as its No. 53 out of Cicero Yard. Eastward, a BAKCT came out of the west with connections for CNW's KMDWA, followed by a fast-moving LACHF with some additional business for Milwaukee Road. The bulk of this train became BN's No. 54 for a speedy ride to the switching crews in Cicero. Milwaukee Road's No. 226 contributed to fill up this day's BSMFF. Then Norfolk and Western chimed in with some connecting tonnage out of Decatur, Illinois, on KD18, to be inserted into a CHLAF consist, while Cotton Belt reciprocated on the LACHF with cars for the trainline of TC4 heading out of Kansas City for Bellevue, Ohio.

Additionally, Rio Grande and SP have teamed to expedite bridge traffic between Ogden, Utah, and Kansas City. Typically this involves a through train each way daily across the Rockies and onto the plains, where D&RGW utilizes the Central Kansas Division of MoPac to move from Pueblo, Colorado, to Kansas City—another of the concessions made under the UP-MP partnership. On top of this there is interchange at Herington, Kansas, between SP-D&RGW, resulting in through Kansas City Division trains doing a bit of switching at the same time crews are swapped at this mid-Kansas division point.

The surges in train action that sometimes affect any major terminal have a greater effect upon Armourdale than most. That's because the former Rock Island yard sits at one extreme of a very long road. Unlike Houston, El Paso, Los Angeles or Eugene, there are not a lot of units coming in from several directions, consequently engines cannot be borrowed for a few hours or assignments stepped up, because more trains are due shortly. What's headed into Kansas City from East St. Louis or from Tucumcari is it, and none of those places is a major maintenance facility either, where spare power can sometimes be had. If unexpected interchange is coming onto the Kansas City Division from other roads, local officials have to scramble or, if necessary, borrow power from connecting roads, a factor which seems habitual.

Bracketed in among Espee motive power combinations are units off

Highball. It's late on a June day in 1985 as a westbound symbol stretches slack beyond Herington, Kansas. Several cars have been set out for pickup by a westbound Rio Grande train, the latter road having trackage rights over MoPac iron at this point.

the Katy, BN, Santa Fe, UP and Rio Grande, at least on this end of the railroad. For with all the mingling of trains through Kansas City, it is expected that locomotives would follow suit.

To illustrate what can happen, consider this Saturday scene we've been discussing. Arriving from Los Angeles, the LACHT is headed up by two BN SD-40s and two Santa Fe SD-40s. Other than a caboose, there's little to suggest whose railroad is in charge. Since this train will be cut up at Armourdale, and will continue as parts of other lines, the power is cut off. A bare 20 minutes suffice for sand and fuel, then it's back on the point of a westbound ASLAA (Alton & Southern-Los Angeles Autos) all the way to the Coast.

Consider the demand upon these machines!

Heading westbound out of Armourdale Yard puts SP trains on board Union Pacific for the initial 60-odd miles of Kansas Division. Then there are five end-to-end Cotton Belt subdivisions that eventually connect with original Espee iron at Tucumcari. Although Subdivision 3 of the Kansas City Division is officially in existence at Armourdale, it's only at S.J. Junction outside Topeka where Cotton Belt finds its own roadbed, entering 60 miles of single track with CTC navigation—all that exists on this outpost of the empire.

When the California-based railroad spent heavily on resuscitating the

182

Rock, traffic control facilities would have seemed a natural. In lieu of it other changes were implemented. New block signals were installed, of course, but the real difference between this line and other past systemwide installations was an operational pattern known as Direct Traffic Control.

DTC is a contemporary train control program placed on certain SP lines which in prior years would be more traditionally characterized as train order territory. Existing where there is no CTC, DTC groups a series of consecutive sidings into "blocks" of varied length, generally 10 to 20 miles. A train is given exclusive occupancy of each block, communicated by radio from the dispatcher to a single member-designate of the crew. Authority is granted for the next, and the next, until a meet is in order. Where local moves are concerned, it's necessary to scuttle into a siding to await passage of mainline trains.

This modern-day version of the old staff system is backed up by automatic block signals throughout, giving a dispatcher considerable flexibility over printed train orders with their often-rigid instructions. These days there are few train order offices open, making flimsies difficult to alter as circumstances of train operations vary. The radio of course is just the tool for this scene, but until lately there has been a great reticence on the part of federal regulatory authorities about its place in setting up meets.

Net result in Kansas is a system of train control which lies between the total smoothness of a high-cost, dynamic CTC installation and that of a more time-consuming, labor-intensive, train order system. In today's system backup safety is provided by block signals, and the entire line between Herington and Tucumcari is naturally protected given its status. If in some rare circumstances there was a radioed misunderstanding, block signals would provide a potential of failsafe mode.

Subdivision 4, 127 miles of high-speed single track across the open plains of Kansas from Herington to Pratt, illustrates how DTC has been established. First you'll notice that near some—not all—siding switches prominent metal signs display block identification, named for the siding itself. This system is specified in SP's operating rulebook as RULE 265, showing nine individual blocks on the subdivision, limits of which are precisely defined.

A typical block averages 15 to 18 miles in this territory. The Ramona block just west of Herington, for example, "extends from clearance point east switch Waldeck siding, MP 197.8 and clearance point east switch Ramona siding, MP 172.3." This particular block encompasses 20 miles of single track, with two intermediate sidings that are not intended for meets, but which like most such affairs on the ex-RI, have grain elevators.

There's another facet of this DTC system, especially here on the onetime Rock Island, that is not so apparent. Several years prior to its end, the midwestern road had an operating manager who, although saddled with limited resources, had great vision: he had many sidings extended out

The 5110 is assigned to local work at Dalhart, Texas, where the proximity to Kansas and the grain trade is readily apparent.

to 9,000 feet. Today there is one of these long passing tracks about every 15 to 20 miles over the entire 463 miles between Herington and Tucumcari. Because of the lengths of SP's important freights, these sidings have proved to be exceedingly valuable.

□

Western Kansas has at times been described as an expansive inland sea, flat like an ocean with waves generated on miles of golden wheat. To everything else SP does and has done the annual Great Plains wheat harvest has become a part of the railroad's thinking processes.

Since Rock Island's departure, the Kansas Division has become pretty much a large-motored locomotive domain, with SD45s and 40s dominant until the arrival of GP40-2s and B-30-7s. The need for grain harvest locals in summer, in addition to the solid through runs, has brought an influx of 7700 class and 4800 class four-axled locomotives. Admittedly there haven't been too many grain harvests under SP tutelage, but during the summer of '86 that was the pattern that emerged.

Long stacks of grey flannel hoppers labeled "Cotton Belt," 9,000-foot sidings, DTC and ex-Rock Island trackage have provided Southern Pacific with another new dimension for the 1980s.

Had Southern Pacific-Santa Fe become a reality the Kansas Division would possibly have taken on even greater significance. At first the money pumped into ex-RI roadbed would seem redundant, as SP's long-coveted shortcut to the Pacific Coast would duplicate Uncle John's routing. However, this fails to take into account a Santa Fe bottleneck of sorts south out of Kansas City, at least in comparison to the several hundred miles of immaculately groomed and signaled double track which flows like an unrestricted pipeline between Belen, N.M., and San Bernardino, Calif.

184

The rumor had Santa Fe cutting into Cotton Belt's K.C. Division at Hutchinson to provide a bit of traffic relief on the transcontinental run, rejoining the original routing at Vaughn, N.M., where the two roads now cross one another.

It would have fit very neatly into a single gigantic railroad as a map exercise would show.

It apparently isn't going to happen under any conceivable circumstance but either way Kansas Division's future is bright, strategically positioned as part of Southern Pacific's far-flung empire or whatever comes along to substitute for the now shunned merger.

It is now something that the Rock Island never was.

Trailing behind this duo of GP-38-2s are some 40-odd empty hoppers being moved from Kansas City down into mid-Kansas for distribution to grain storage facilities.

185

Opposite: The SP uses Rio Grande as a bridge route between Ogden and Herington, Kansas, exposing its locomotive roster to one additional set of tough mountains, the Rockies.

Besides the block signals which control trains, the Directed Traffic Control System is in use on the Kansas Division with the blocks identified by signs such as this.

North of Dalhart, an eastbound piggybacker trundles across the high span bridge over the Canadian River, a yawning chasm in an otherwise flat, featureless section of SP's roadbed.

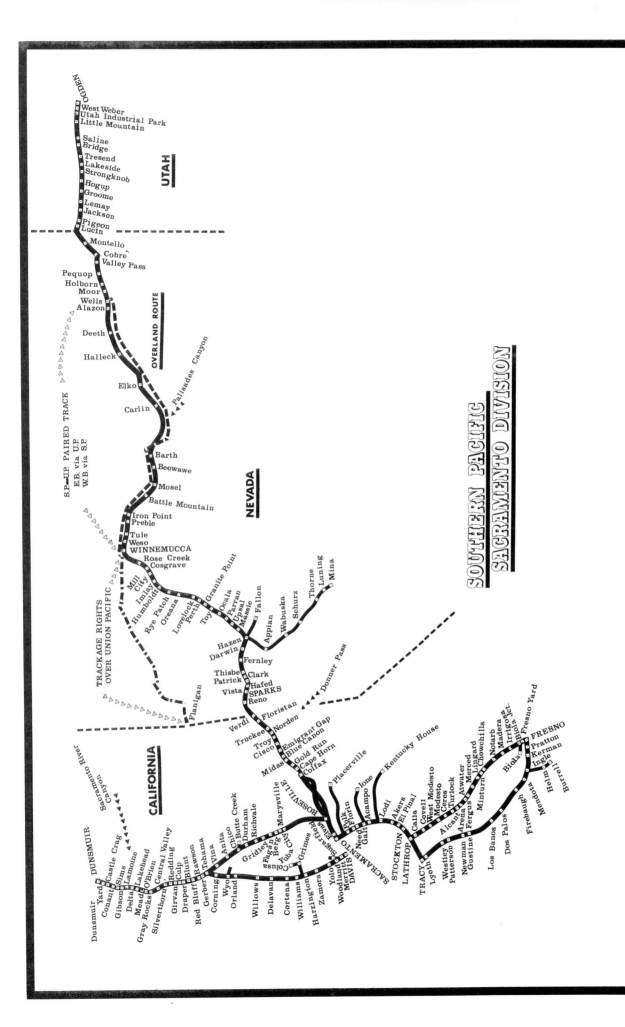

SOUTHERN PACIFIC
SACRAMENTO DIVISION

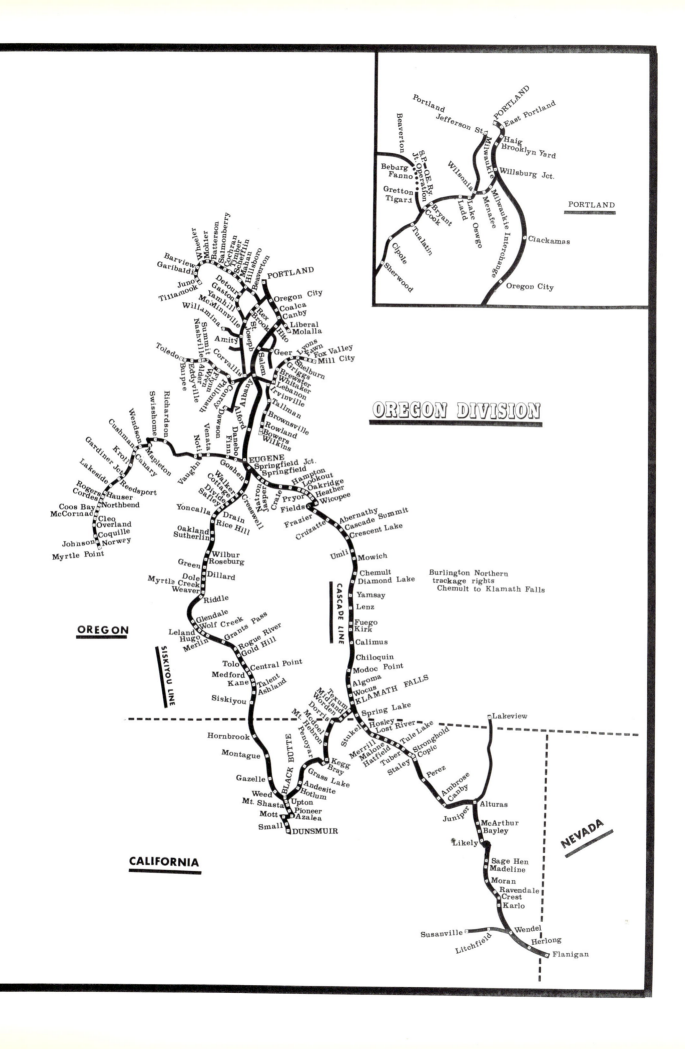

OREGON DIVISION

PORTLAND

Portland
Jefferson St.
Beaverton
Beberg
Fanno
Gretton
Tigard
SP-OE Ry.
Jt. Operation
Bryant
Cook
Cipole
Sherwood
Tualatin
PORTLAND
East Portland
Haig
Brooklyn Yard
Willsburg Jct.
Willamette
Menafee
Lake Oswego
Ladd
Milwaukie Interchange
Clackamas
Oregon City
Wilsonia
Wilsonia

PORTLAND

Barview
Garibaldi
Juno
Tillamook
Willamina
Toledo
Eddyville
Buipee
Nashville
Alder
Summit
Wren
Philomath
Corvallis
Wheeler
Mohler
Batterson
Salmonberry
Cochran
Scheffin
Timber
Mahan
Hillsboro
Beaverton
Detour
Gaston
Yamhill
McMinnville
Amity
Joseph
St.
Brook
Rex
Hito
PORTLAND
Oregon City
Coalca
Canby
Liberal
Molalla
Lyons
Fawn
Fox Valley
Mill City
Geer
Salem
Shelburn
Griggs
Brewster
Whitaker
Lebanon
Irvinville
Tallman
Brownsville
Rowland
Bowers
Wilkins

Richardson
Swisshome
Wendson
Cushman
Krof
Gardiner Jct.
Canary
Mapleton
Lakeside
Reedsport
Rogers
Cordes
Hauser
Northbend
Coos Bay
McCormac
Cleo
Overland
Coquille
Johnson
Norwey
Myrtle Point

Noti
Vaughn
Venata
Walker
Cottage
Divide
Saffey
Goshen
Norton
Jasper
Creswell
Crate
Pryor
Fields
Frazier
Cruzatte
Danebo
Finn
EUGENE
Springfield Jct.
Springfield
Hampton
Lookout
Oakridge
Heather
Wicopee
Abernathy
Cascade Summit
Crescent Lake

Yoncalla
Drain
Rice Hill
Oakland
Sutherlin
Wilbur
Roseburg
Green
Dole
Dillard
Myrtle Creek
Weaver
Riddle
Glendale
Wolf Creek
Leland
Hugo
Merlin
Grants Pass
Rogue River
Gold Hill
Tolo
Central Point
Medford
Kane
Talent
Ashland
Siskiyou

Umli
Mowich
Chemult
Diamond Lake
Yamsay
Lenz
Fuego
Kirk
Calimus
Chiloquin
Modoc Point
Algoma
Wocus
KLAMATH FALLS
Spring Lake

Burlington Northern
trackage rights
Chemult to Klamath Falls

CASCADE LINE

OREGON

SISKIYOU LINE

Hornbrook
Montague
Gazelle
Weed
Mt. Shasta
Mott
Small
Upton
Pioneer
Azalea
DUNSMUIR
BLACK BUTTE
Penoyar
Mt. Hebron
Grass Lake
Andesite
Hotlum
Kegg
Bray
Dorris
Macdoel
Worden
Midland
Texum
Stukel
Hosley
Lost River
Merrill
Malone
Hatfield
Tuber
Staley
Tule Lake
Stronghold
Copic
Perez
Ambrose
Canby
Juniper
Likely
KLAMATH FALLS

Lakeview
Alturas
McArthur
Bayley
Sage Hen
Madeline
Moran
Ravendale
Crest
Karlo
Susanville
Litchfield
Wendel
Herlong
Flanigan

NEVADA

CALIFORNIA

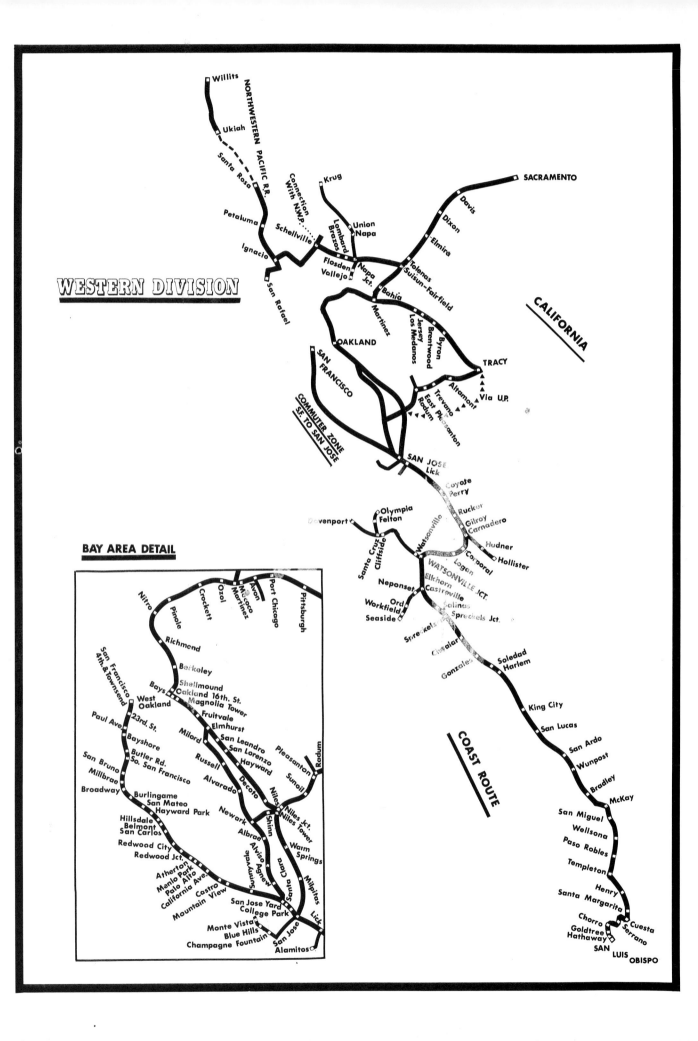

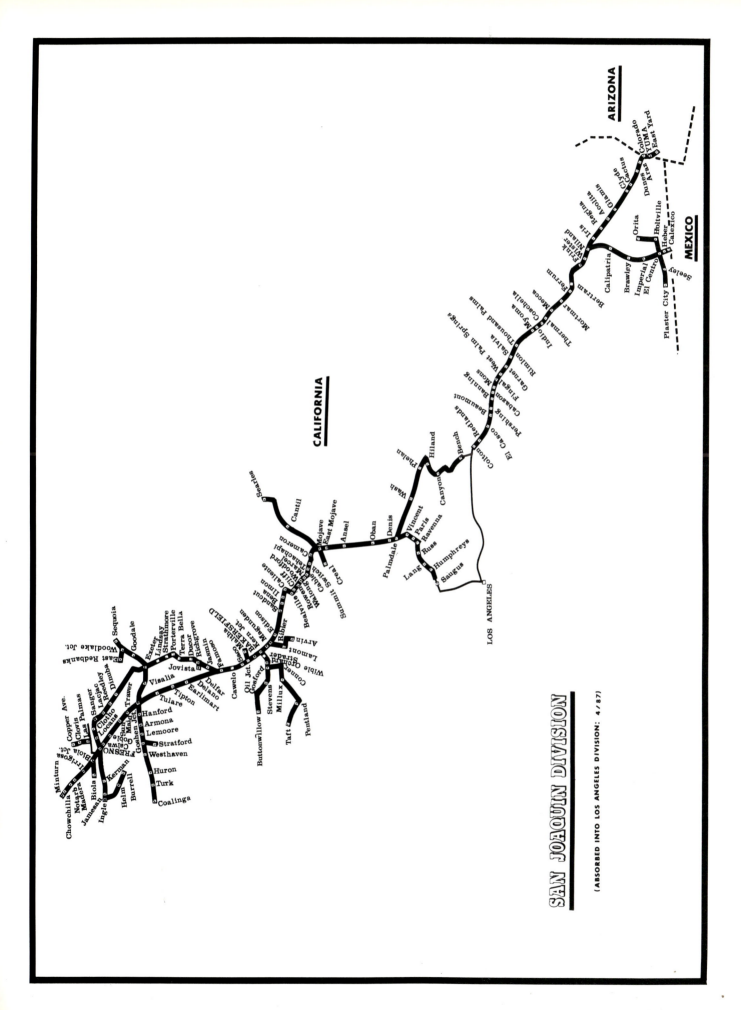

SAN JOAQUIN DIVISION

(ABSORBED INTO LOS ANGELES DIVISION: 4/87)

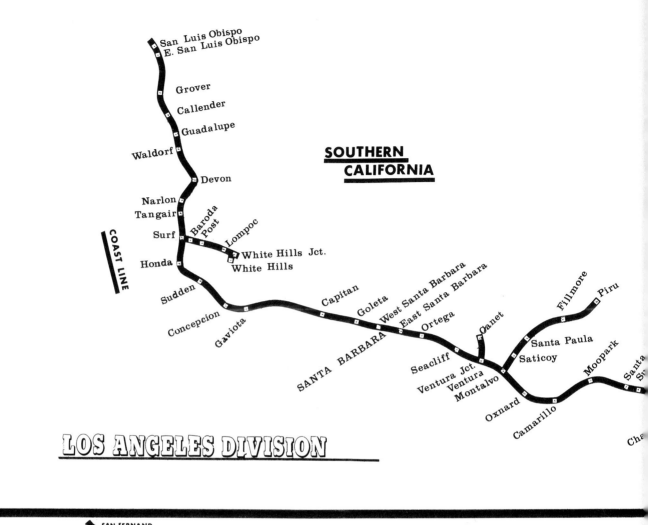

SOUTHERN CALIFORNIA

San Luis Obispo
E. San Luis Obispo
Grover
Callender
Guadalupe
Waldorf
Devon
Narlon
Tangair
Surf
Baroda
Post
Lompoc
White Hills Jct.
White Hills
Honda
Sudden
Concepcion
Gaviota
Capitan
Goleta
West Santa Barbara
East Santa Barbara
Ortega
SANTA BARBARA
Seacliff
Ventura Jct.
Ventura
Montalvo
Oxnard
Camarillo
Ganet
Saticoy
Santa Paula
Fillmore
Piru
Moorpark
Santa S...
Cha...

COAST LINE

LOS ANGELES DIVISION

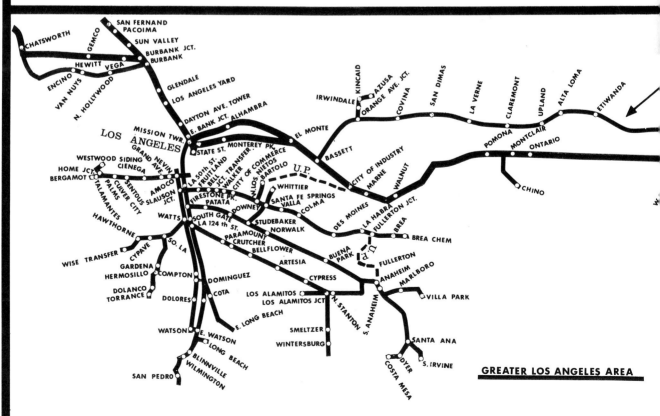

GREATER LOS ANGELES AREA

CHATSWORTH
GEMCO
SAN FERNAND
PACOIMA
SUN VALLEY
BURBANK JCT.
BURBANK
HEWITT
VEGA
ENCINO
VAN NUYS
N. HOLLYWOOD
GLENDALE
LOS ANGELES YARD
DAYTON AVE. TOWER
E. BANK JCT. ALHAMBRA
MISSION TWR.
LOS ANGELES
STATE ST. MONTEREY PK.
EL MONTE
IRWINDALE
KINCAID
AZUSA
ORANGE AVE. JCT.
COVINA
SAN DIMAS
LA VERNE
CLAREMONT
UPLAND
ALTA LOMA
ETIWANDA
GRAND NEVIN
WESTWOOD SIDING
CIENEGA
HOME JCT.
BERGAMOT
SENTOUS
AMOCO
CULVER CITY
PALMS
TALAMANTES
HAWTHORNE
WISE TRANSFER
GARDENA
HERMOSILLO
COMPTON
DOLANCO
TORRANCE
DOLORES
WATSON
E. WATSON
LONG BEACH
BLINNVILLE
WILMINGTON
SAN PEDRO
LA 50th ST.
FRUITLAND
BELL TRANSFER
JCT. WALKER
FIRESTONE PK.
PATATA
SLAUSON JCT.
WATTS
SO. LA
CYPAVE
LA 124 th ST.
SOUTH GATE
PARAMOUNT
CRUTCHER
BELLFLOWER
ARTESIA
DOMINGUEZ
COTA
E. LONG BEACH
CITY OF COMMERCE
N. LOS NIETOS
BARTOLO
WHITTIER
SANTA FE SPRINGS
VALLA
DOWNEY
STUDEBAKER
NORWALK
U.P.
COLMA
DES MOINES
BASSETT
CITY OF INDUSTRY
MARNE
WALNUT
LA HABRA
FULLERTON JCT.
BREA
BREA CHEM
BUENA PARK
FULLERTON
ANAHEIM
S. ANAHEIM
MARLBORO
VILLA PARK
CYPRESS
LOS ALAMITOS
LOS ALAMITOS JCT.
N. STANTON
SMELTZER
WINTERSBURG
COSTA MESA
DYER
SANTA ANA
S. IRVINE
POMONA
MONTCLAIR
ONTARIO
CHINO

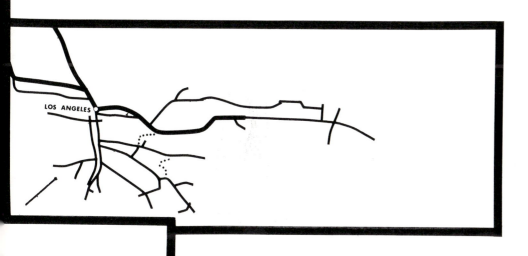

LOS ANGELES

NCH

OLTON

TUCSON DIVISION

GOLDEN STATE ROUTE

TUCUMARI
Hargis
Montoya
Palomas
Newkirk
Cuervo
Los Tanos
SANTA ROSA
Arabella
Pastura
Leoncito
Yeoncito
Vaughn
Corona
Gallinas
Ancho
Robsart
CARRIZOZO
Polly
Three Rivers
ALAMOGORDO
Omlee
Dunes
Orogrande
Desert
Newman
Tobin
Fort Bliss
Bunsen
Planeport
Anapra
EL PASO
Lizard
Strauss
Lanark
Afton
Dona Aden
Akela
Carne
Sage
DEMING
Tunis
Gage
Wilna
Separ
Lisbon
Ulmoris
Mondel
LORDSBURG
Summit
Stein
Duncan
Fox
South Siding
CLIFTON
Vanar
San Simon
Olga
Bowie
Luzena
Raso
DOUGLAS
Calumet
Naco
Bisbee Jct.
Bigbee
Dragoon
Sibyl
Tully
Fenner
Benson
Cochise
Willcox
Luzena
Safford
Pima
Cork
Geronimo
San Carlos
Cutter
Globe
Burch
Miami
Winkelman
Hayden
Ray Jct.
Florence
Randolph
Coolidge
Picacho
Red Rock
Toltec
Casa Grande
Bon
Maricopa
Mobile
Estrella
Shawmut
Gila
Bosque
Liberty
Buckeye
Dixie
Smurr
Arlington
Theba
Piedra
Saddle
Gillespie
Sentinel
Stanwix
Azteca
Stoval
Mohawk
Kofa
Roll
Colfred
Noah
Wellton
Dome
Kinter
Fortuna

PFE Yard
Marsh
Curtiss
Chamiso
Mescal
Pantano
Benson Jct.
Fairbank
Lewis Springs
Wilmot
Vail
PFE Yard
TUCSON
Irvington
Jaynes
Rialto
Sahuarita
Canoa
Amado
Calabasas
Nogales
Wymola
Magma
Queen Creek
Rittenhouse
Higley
McQueen
Enid
Serape
Dock

SUNSET ROUTE

ARIZONA
NEW MEXICO
TEXAS
MEXICO
CALIFORNIA

TUCSON and VICINITY
Rillito
Plata
Sabino
Cortaro
Kilo
Jaynes
Stockham
Petrie
TUCSON
PFE Yard

PHOENIX and VICINITY
Gilbert
Mesa
McQueen
Tremaine
Falfa
Chandler
Pozo
West Chandler
Normal Jct.
Peterson
Helena
Tempe
Kendall
Torrea
Auction
Yeso
Aristuo
PHOENIX
Phoenix Yard
Campo
Pipeola
Cotpro
Fowler
Atlsr
Tolleson
Cashion
Litchfield
Litchfield Jct.
Salt River
Gila River

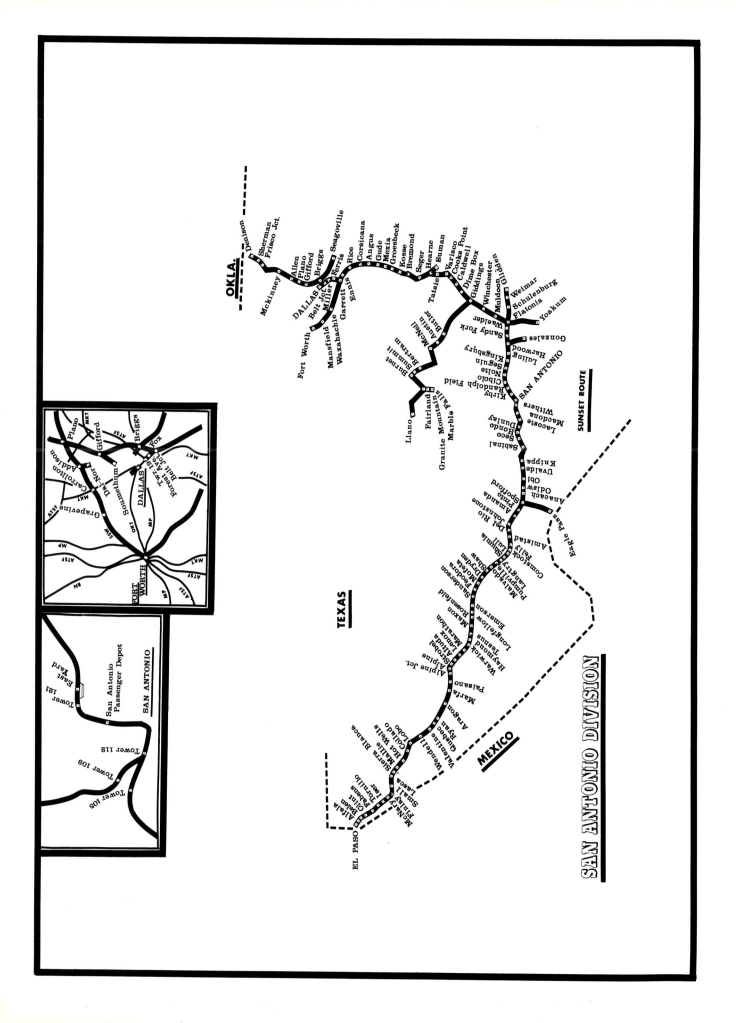

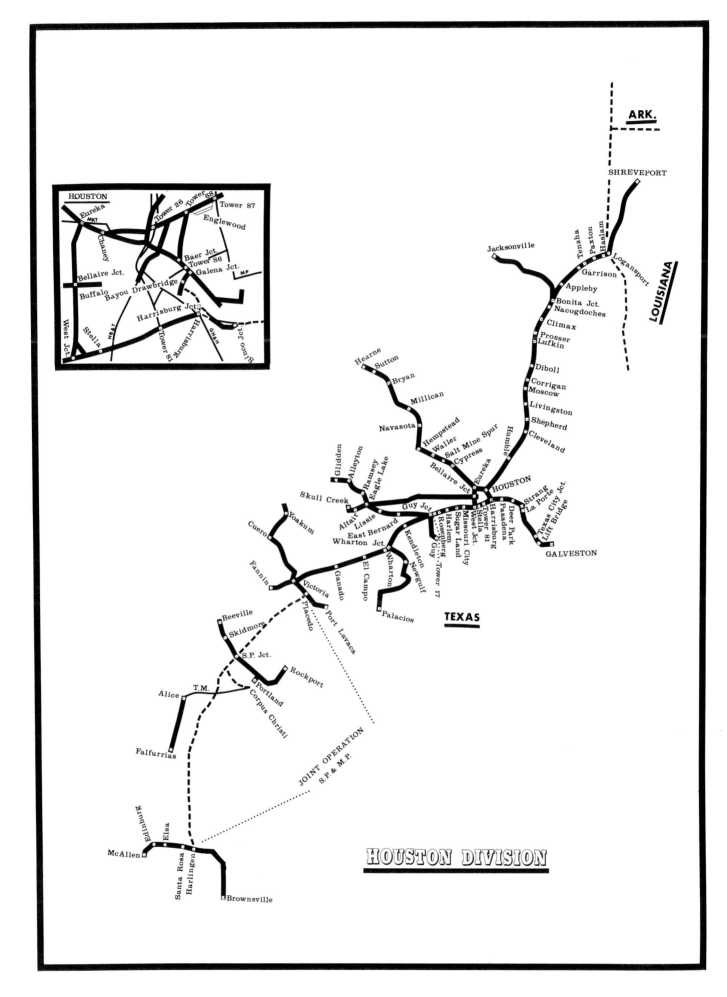

HOUSTON DIVISION

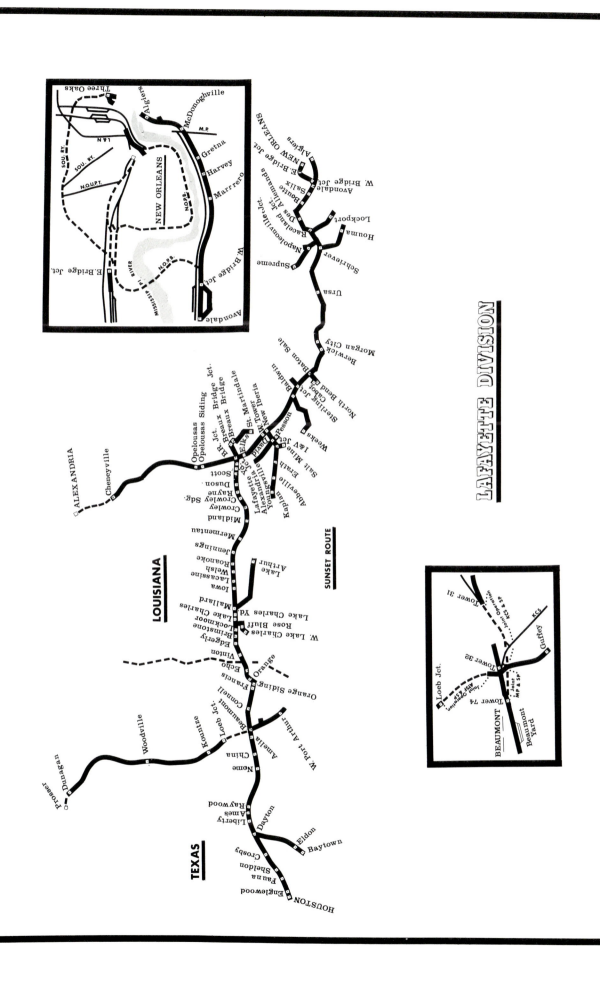

LAFAYETTE DIVISION

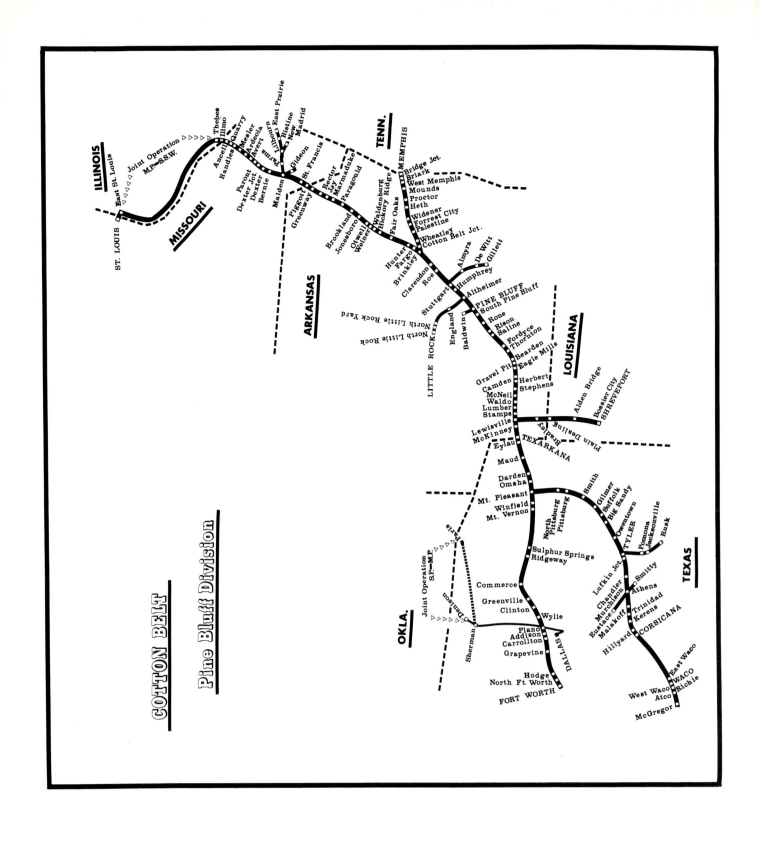

COTTON BELT

Pine Bluff Division

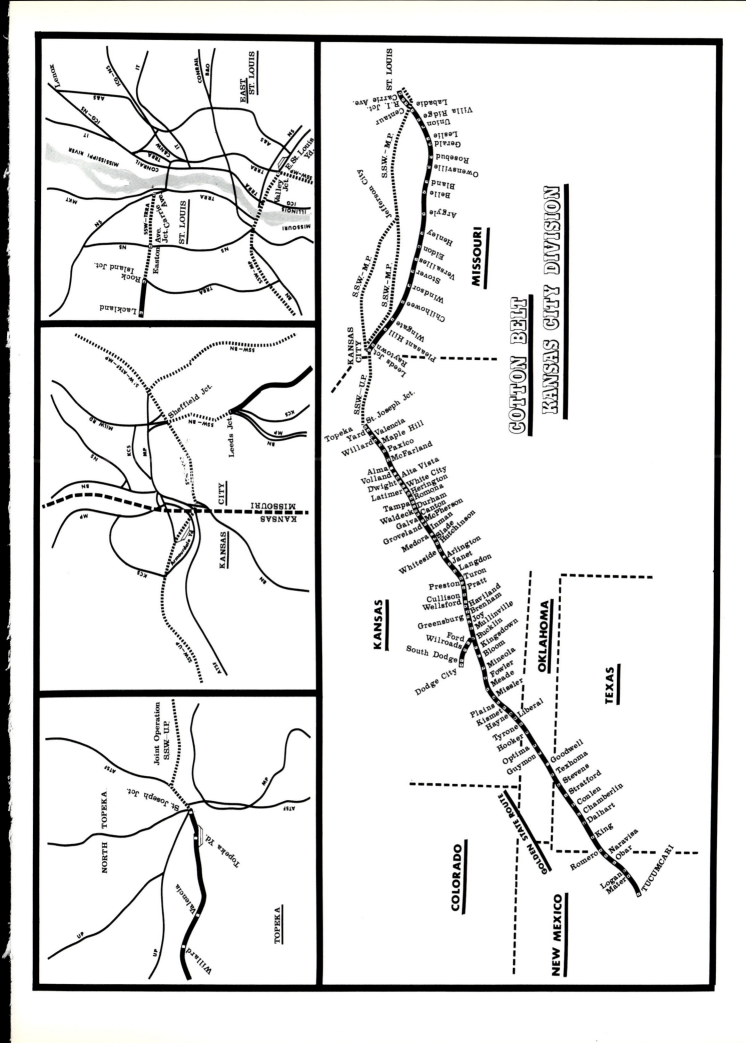